UTOPIA

An Elusive Vision

✤

TWAYNE'S MASTERWORK STUDIES

Robert Lecker, General Editor

UTOPIA

An Elusive Vision

✤

Alistair Fox

TWAYNE PUBLISHERS ◆ NEW YORK

Maxwell Macmillan Canada ◆ Toronto

Maxwell Macmillan International ◆ New York Oxford Singapore Sydney

Twayne's Masterwork Studies No. 103

Twayne Publishers
Macmillan Publishing Company
866 Third Avenue
New York, New York 10022

Maxwell Macmillan Canada, Inc.
1200 Eglinton Avenue East
Suite 200
Don Mills, Ontario M3C 3N1

Macmillan Publishing Company is a part of the Maxwell Communication
Group of Companies.

Library of Congress Cataloging-in-Publication Data

Fox, Alistair.
Utopia : an elusive vision / by Alistair Fox.
p. cm. — (Twayne's masterwork studies ; 103)
Includes bibliographical references and index.
ISBN 0-8057-9419-0 — ISBN 0-8057-8570-1 (pbk.)
1. More, Thomas, Sir, Saint, 1478–1535. Utopia. I. Title.
HX810.5.Z6F68 1993
335'.02—dc20
92-23396
CIP

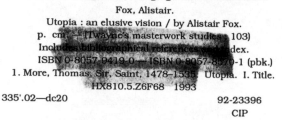

For Alison Heatherbell Fox

Contents

Illustrations

Note on the References and Acknowledgments

References to *Utopia* are to volume 4 of the standard *Yale Edition of the Complete Works of St. Thomas More,* edited by Edward Surtz and J. H. Hexter (New Haven, Conn., and London: Yale University Press, 1965), and are cited in the text by page and line numbers (i.e., "221/13–14" means p. 221, lines 13 to 14). Critical commentary included in volume 4 is cited by page number and preceded by *CW*4. Unless stated otherwise, references to More's other works are to the respective volumes of the 14-volume *Yale Edition* and are cited as *CW* and volume number.

Utopia was originally written in Latin, which causes problems for anyone writing critically about it, for there can be very few commentators who will be prepared to agree with the translation given by any other. Although its Latin text is definitive, some of the English translations *The Yale Edition* provides are stilted, tendentious, and even garbled. For the ease of the reader, I, for the most part, have quoted from this English text; occasionally, however, I have preferred to give my own translations, in which cases the original Latin is given in brackets immediately following the translated English.

I am grateful to Dr. Seymour House for helpful comments arising from his reading of an early version of this work, and to Abbé Germain Marc'hadour, who sacrificed considerable time from a busy schedule to peruse the manuscript during his most recent visit to the Antipodes. The book has benefited from their attention, although any remaining errors in judgment are in fact my own.

Finally, I wish to acknowledge the following persons and institutions for granting permission to reproduce works of art:

The Frick Collection, New York City, for *Sir Thomas More*, by Hans Holbein the Younger.

The British Library, London, for *Henry VIII in Council*, by Jacob Faber after Hans Holbein.

The Bodleian Library, Oxford, for the title page from Thomas More, *De optimo reip. Statu deque noua insula Utopia*, 1518 (Shelfmark Byw.Q.2.9).

Galleria Nazionale d'Arte Antica in Palazzo Barberini, Rome, for *Desiderius Erasmus*, by Quentin Massys.

The Courtauld Institute of Art, University of London, for *Peter Giles (Petrus Aegidius)*, by Quentin Massys (private collection).

Sir Thomas More, by Hans Holbein the Younger.
The Frick Collection, New York City

Chronology: Sir Thomas More's Life and Works

1478 or 1477	Thomas More born in London on 7 February to John More, a judge on the King's Bench, and Agnes (née Graunger) More.
1485	The last Yorkist king, Richard III, is defeated and killed at Bosworth Field; Henry Tudor ascends to throne as King Henry VII.
ca. 1490–1492	Thomas More serves as page in the household of John Morton, archbishop of Canterbury and lord chancellor, later cardinal. More impresses spectators with his talent for improvising roles for himself in dramatic performances.
ca. 1492–1494	Studies liberal arts at Oxford University.
ca. 1494–1501	Studies law at the Inns of Court—first New Inn, then Lincoln's Inn.
1499	Meets Desiderius Erasmus during the Dutchman's first visit to England.
1504	Elected to Parliament, incurring the wrath of Henry VII because of his opposition to the king's request for a subsidy.
ca. 1500–1504	Engages in vigils, fasting, and prayer with the Carthusian monks in the Charterhouse of London. Delivers lectures on Saint Augustine's *City of God* in Grocyn's church; composes poems in English.

1504 or 1505	Marries Jane Colt.
1505	Daughter Margaret born. Erasmus makes second visit to England; he and More enter into friendly rivalry to translate some dialogues of Lucian of Samosata from Greek to Latin. (The translations are published together in Paris in 1506.)
ca. 1508	Visits the Universities of Paris and Louvain for a time.
1509	Henry VII dies; Henry VIII ascends to throne and marries Catherine of Aragon. More writes congratulatory verses in Latin to present to the new king. Erasmus writes *The Praise of Folly* (published in 1511) while staying at More's house.
1510–1518	More serves as an undersheriff of London.
1511	Jane Colt dies; More marries Alice Middleton within a month of Jane's death.
1512–1513	England at war with France.
1513	Niccolò Machiavelli writes *The Prince* (published in 1532).
ca. 1513– 1518	More writes *The History of King Richard III* (published in 1557).
1515	Commissioned by Henry VIII on 7 May to go on a diplomatic mission to Flanders to negotiate with representatives of the Holy Roman emperor, Charles V. Writes book 2 of *Utopia* from May to October. In October defends Erasmus's *Praise of Folly* and humanist learning in his *Letter to Maarten Dorp*.
1516	*Utopia* published in Louvain in December. (The second edition is published in Paris in 1517 and the third and fourth editions in Basel in March and November of 1518, together with More's *Epigrammata*.)

1517	More enters the service of Henry VIII, becoming a member of the Royal Council. In October Martin Luther draws up 95 theses for debate, which herald the onset of the Reformation.
1518	More again defends humanistic learning in his *Letter to Oxford University*.
1520	Luther writes and publishes *The Babylonian Captivity of the Church*.
ca. 1521	The Duke of Buckingham is executed; More writes *A Treatise on the Four Last Things* (published in 1557).
1522–1523	Writes *Responsio ad Lutherum* (Reply to Luther), a defense of Henry VIII against Luther's attack on the king's *Assertio septem sacramentorum*, which proclaims the sanctity of tradition in the Catholic Church and the power of the pope.
1523	Serves as speaker of the House of Commons.
1525	Appointed chancellor of the duchy of Lancaster.
1528	Commissioned on 7 March by Cuthbert Tunstall, the bishop of London, to write works in the vernacular to refute Lutheran heresies. Writes in rapid succession *A Dialogue Concerning Heresies* (1529), *Supplication of Souls* (1529), *Confutation of Tyndale's Answer* (1532–33), *Letter Impugning the Erronious Writings of John Frith* (1532), *Apology of Sir Thomas More, Knight* (1533), *Debellation of Salem and Bizance* (1533), and *Answer to a Poisoned Book which a Nameless Heretic hath called The Supper of the Lord* (1533).
1529	Succeeds Cardinal Wolsey as lord chancellor.
1532	Resigns as lord chancellor on 16 May in response to *Submission of the Clergy*, a document in which the English bishops surrender their independent legislative power to the king.
1533	Henry VIII marries Anne Boleyn and crowns her queen; More refuses to attend the coronation.

1534   Writes *A Treatise on the Passion* (1557). Parliament passes the Act of Succession on 23 March, declaring Henry's marriage to Catherine of Aragon null from the beginning and his marriage to Anne Boleyn lawful, extending the definition of treason to cover attacks on the marriage and binding all English subjects to swear faithful obedience to the king's heirs by Queen Anne. On 13 April More refuses to swear the Oath of Succession and on 17 April is imprisoned in the Tower of London.

1534–1535   Writes *A Dialogue of Comfort against Tribulation* (1553) and *De tristitia Christi* (On the sadness of Christ; 1557) while imprisoned.

1535   Is tried and convicted of treason on 1 July: is beheaded on Tower Hill on 6 July.

1551   The first English translation, by Ralph Robinson, of *Utopia* is published.

1557   More's collected works in English are published by his nephew William Rastell as *The Workes of Syr Thomas More Knyght, Sometyme Lorde Chauncellor of England, Wrytten by him in the Englysh Tonge.*

1565–1566   More's collected works in Latin are published in Louvain.

1935   More is canonized by the Roman Catholic Church on 19 May.

LITERARY AND
HISTORICAL CONTEXT

✤

≈ ≈ ≈≈ God ſaue the Kyng. ≈ ≈ ≈

Henry VIII in Council, Jacob Faber after Hans Holbein, printed in Hall's *Chronicle,* 1548. *The British Library, London.* This woodcut shows the council More was invited to join on his return to England from the Netherlands. It is similar to the council in which Hythlodaeus imagines himself offering "utopian" advice to a king in book 1 of *Utopia.*

1

Humanism and Reform

On 7 May 1515 Thomas More, a leading citizen, lawyer, and under-sheriff of the City of London, received a commission from King Henry VIII to join an important diplomatic mission to Flanders, his brief being to renegotiate certain commercial treaties made during the reign of Henry's predecessor, Henry VII. As he left the shores of England little did he know that the negotiations would be pro-tracted for over half a year. By 21 July the talks had stalled, and More found that he had time to kill while waiting for them to resume (which they did in late October). It was during these three months of enforced leisure in Bruges that he wrote the larger part of *Utopia*, the story of his imaginary commonwealth.

UTOPIA AND THE DRIVE FOR REFORM

In the summer of 1515 Europe seemed on the brink of a new age, and it is to a prevailing spirit of expectation that *Utopia* responds. During the late Middle Ages many institutions were showing signs of exhaustion. Scholastic learning had become arid and obsessed with trivialities. Europe had been ravaged for over a century by wars, as a result of the petty ambitions and greed of irresponsible rulers. Most seriously, the Church had become riddled with cor-ruption. As Desiderius Erasmus satirically scoffed in *The Praise of Folly* (1511), contemporary pontiffs, instead of being the vicars of Christ, had become the deadliest enemies of the Church, striving

3

ceaselessly after wealth, honors, and countless pleasures, and even stooping to fight with fire and sword to preserve their privileges.[1] By the end of the fifteenth century almost everyone felt the need for renovation and reform, and to men like More and Erasmus, humanism seemed to promise it.

From as early as 1488, Erasmus, the leading scholar of his day and a figure of international importance, had systematically promoted a program for reform based on the ideals and practices of Renaissance humanism. Humanism was a distinct ideology that originated in the Italian universities during the late fifteenth century in opposition to the traditional values of the medieval Schoolmen. The term *humanist* was used to refer to teachers and students of classical learning and literature, particularly to those who favored a new curricular emphasis on grammar, rhetoric, ethics, history, and poetry as studied in the classical texts of Greece and Rome rather than the old Scholastic emphasis on logic, natural philosophy, and metaphysics as studied in the "blotterature" (as More's mentor, John Colet, termed it) of the Middle Ages.[2] Erasmus believed fervently that humanist learning could act as a powerful force for reform; the classical sources could yield a purified morality that, dressed up in the finery of classical rhetoric and eloquence, could be presented all the more persuasively. In particular, Erasmus sought tirelessly to convert those in a position of influence to the new ideas: the rulers, the preachers, and the schoolmasters.

By 1515 the reformist optimism of the Erasmus and his fellow humanists was at its height. The most powerful countries of Europe were coming under the control of younger rulers who seemed highly responsive to humanist ideas. England's Henry VIII had succeeded his austere father in 1509 and had shown himself to be a friend to the arts. Similarly, Francis I had ascended to France's throne in 1515, and Charles V, for whom Erasmus had written his treatise *The Education of a Christian Prince* (1516), would soon be chosen emperor over the Habsburg dominions. The new grammar-school curriculum that Erasmus had devised for John Colet's school at St. Paul's had furnished a pattern that would influence generations of future schoolboys, and in England, especially, humanist studies had captured the universities, as the poet John Skelton was to complain:

4

Plautus in his comedies a chyld shall now reherse,
And medyll with Quintylyan in his Declamacyons,
That *Pety Caton* can scantly construe a verse,
With, "*Aveto*" in *Greco*, and such solempne salutacyons,
Can skantly the tensis of his conjugacyons;
Settyng theyr myndys so moche of eloquens,
That of theyr scole maters lost is the hole sentens.[3]

Perhaps the chief weapon in the humanists' armory was the new
Latin translation of the New Testament with its parallel Greek text,
known as the *Novum instrumentum*, that Erasmus had been
preparing to rescue the simple message of the Gospels from the
casuistry of the theologians. With this translation he hoped to fos-
ter piety by making the "philosophy of Christ" more widely known.
The international humanist community to which More belonged
thus had every reason to believe that Europe was about to fall
under the sway of rulers who would govern according to the purified ethical and religious values they had been trying to propagate,
and that a new golden age was about to dawn as a result. In any
consideration of *Utopia* it is important to keep these hopes and
expectations in mind, for More's imaginary commonwealth was
written as a means of contemplating them.

Humanism itself was a manifestation of something still larger:
a general renovation of the human spirit and its creative impulses
that started in Italy in the second half of the fourteenth century
and spread north across Europe through the fifteenth and sixteenth centuries. This is what has come to be known as "the
Renaissance," and it is visible particularly in the spectacular
achievements of painters and sculptors such as Leonardo da Vinci,
Michelangelo, Giovanni Lorenzo Bernini, and Sandro Botticelli in
the South, and Albrecht Dürer, Pieter Breughel, Lucas Cranach,
and Hans Holbein in the North. Its philosophy is visible in the
resurgence of classical moral philosophy as imitated from the writings of Cicero and Seneca, in the rediscovery of Platonic idealism by
Marsilio Ficino, Giovanni Pico della Mirandola, and other members
of the Florentine academy. It is seen in literary works that articu-
late the moral and political ideals of the new ethos in a style that
achieves new standards of eloquence, whether written in
Latin—such as Ficino's commentary on Plato's *Symposium*—or in
the vernacular—such as Baldassare Castiglione's *Book of the*

Courtier (1528). In short, the arts were flourishing, and many people felt that the horizons of the human mind were expanding.

Some, however, were—ironically and often bitterly—skeptical that Renaissance humanism would be able to deliver all that it promised, since it had to operate in a world where the depravity of human nature was all too obvious. The most notorious expression of this skepticism was Machiavelli's *The Prince* (1532), in which the author, with awesome cynicism, shows what rulers *must* do to succeed politically rather than—as the humanists were proclaiming—what they *ought* to do. Painters as well were sometimes moved to subvert ironically the idealistic images they were presenting. This can be seen in Holbein's *The Ambassadors*, wherein the emblems of harmony and human intellectual achievement are undermined by the presence of emblems of discord and a gruesome memento mori. The peculiar complexity and ambivalence of *Utopia* comes from the fact that More, like Holbein, experienced simultaneously his age's optimistic idealism and its skeptical pessimism.

UTOPIA AND MORE'S LIFE

If the reformist fervor and groundswell of humanist enthusiasm sweeping across Europe was conducive to the writing of *Utopia*, so too were the circumstances of More's own life. Since being plucked away from Oxford University by his father, who believed his son was wasting his time with liberal studies, More had successfully completed his legal studies at Lincoln's Inn; had gained political experience in the Parliament of 1504; had built up a lucrative private law practice in the City of London, handling civil cases; and had served as an undersheriff of London. He had thus not only gained a fairly high public profile but had also built up a fund of experience that he must have believed equipped him to serve the public good. Moreover, throughout this time he had not lost touch with his humanistic studies. He remained a close friend of Erasmus, collaborating with him to translate some dialogues and declamations of Lucian of Samosata from Greek to Latin and producing a steady stream of epigrams in Latin. He had also begun a most ambitious historical biography, *The History of King Richard III*, written in several Latin versions and an English version to emulate the classical historians, and designed to secure More a reputation on the Continent. More remained deeply committed to the liberal arts, and there is plenty to indicate that he was not averse to the fame and glory that achievement in the arts could bring. He had, however, fallen far behind Erasmus in achievement since the early days when they translated Lucian in friendly rivalry. When the two men met in Bruges in late May of 1515, it is probable that Erasmus revealed to More that he had written a political treatise, *The Education of a Christian Prince.* More must have felt that, given his experience, he could write on such a topic at least as well, if not better. Friendly emulation, then, was a prime motive in the writing of *Utopia.*

There was another compelling personal reason. In 1514 More had successfully defended the pope's interests against the king in a legal case involving an impounded ship.[4] He must have known that, given his high public profile in the City and this demonstration of his skill as an advocate, the chance for political advancement in the King's service was open to him. We can, in fact, discern a paradoxical mingling of contradictory impulses in More, all of which contributed to the peculiar texture and design of *Utopia.* On the one hand, he shared the excitement of other humanists at the prospect of political reform and wanted to contribute to it by offering the fruits of his wisdom and experience; on the other, he had a deeply ingrained pessimism about the extent to which the human condition could be ameliorated. On the one hand, he felt the urge to participate in politics; on the other, he shrank from such participation out of a conviction of its futility. More had a unique vision—complex and multilateral—and a deep psychological complexity at the heart of his being. *Utopia* was written so that More could explore his response to current issues by objectifying his perceptions in the form of an imaginative fiction.

LITERARY AND INTELLECTUAL INFLUENCES

The humanists' enthusiasm for returning to the pagan classics as the founts of wisdom gave a new impetus to political writing in the

Renaissance. The humanists were particularly impressed by Plato's speculations on the ideal society in his *Republic* and *Laws* and by Xenophon's, Isocrates's, and Plutarch's treatises on the ideal ruler and methods of government, which circulated widely during the fifteenth century. As far as political morality was concerned, the humanists depended on the philosophy of the Latin Stoics Cicero and Seneca, which they sought to harmonize with the teachings of Christianity. Their renewed interest in the historical writings of the classical historians should also not be overlooked; the works of Sallust, Suetonius, and Tacitus, in particular, provided an important source of information on the realities of political experience.

This renewed interest in classical political, moral, and historical literature resulted in an outpouring of humanist political treatises throughout the fifteenth century, especially in Italy. These include *De optimo cive* (*On the Best City;* 1504), by Bartolomeo Sacchi de Platina; *De institutione, statu, ac regimine reipublicae* (*On the Institution, State, and Government of a Republic;* 1518), by Francesco Patrizi; and *De optimo statu* (*On the Best State;* ca. 1497), by Filippo Beroaldo. This concern with neoclassical political speculation and admonition later spread to northern Europe, resulting in such works as Erasmus's *The Education of a Christian Prince*, Guillaume Budé's *De l'insitution du prince* (*On the Education of the Prince)*, and More's *Utopia*, all written or published in 1516.

We can safely say that More knew both directly and indirectly the pagan classics and the humanist imitations thereof, even though the influence of these works is felt more often in terms of general preoccupations than precise detail. Plato is by far the most important classical influence on *Utopia*, although More also borrows from Plutarch, Sallust, Tacitus, Cicero, and Seneca.[5] Plato is mentioned more often than any other writer, both in More's text and in the prefatory poem extolling Utopia, which purports to be by one Anemolius, the son of Hythlodaeus's sister (21/1–9). From Plato, More took the idea of contriving an imaginary state founded on ideal justice, together with its central tenet: communism. He also imitated Plato's typical method of arguing by constructing book 1 of *Utopia* as a dialogue.

It is important to note, however, that the differences between *Utopia* and Plato's *Republic* are just as striking as the similarities. More's Utopia is much more practical, realistic, and less abstract

8

than Plato's ideal state. More's imaginary commonwealth is also governed through a system of democratic representation, whereas Plato's community is governed by an aristocratic elite. More thus replaces the notion of descending power with one of ascending power. This is typical of More's method of handling his sources; details and ideas are subsumed within, and filtered through, his own distinctive vision, which makes the identification of specific influences, for the most part, very tenuous.[6]

More's eclecticism and independence of mind make it even more difficult to determine the extent to which he was influenced by the political writings of other humanists. John Colet, his spiritual mentor, had traveled to Italy, and William Grocyn, Thomas Linacre, and William Lily had all studied there. More's own interest in Italian neo-Platonism is attested to by his Latin-to-English translation in about 1504 of *The Life of Pico della Mirandola* (1510), by Pico's nephew. The works of the Italian humanists are thus likely to have been drawn to his attention by his English humanist friends, given their mutual interests.

Erasmus was probably More's most important source of information concerning the works of the continental humanists. He had lived in Italy for three years before hastening to England on the accession of Henry VIII in April 1509, and thereafter he lived in More's house for a time. Equally important, his *Education of a Christian Prince*, of which More was acutely aware while completing *Utopia*, closely imitates the Italian models. Suffice it to say that *Utopia* is fully informed by, and imbued with, the ethos and preoccupations of humanists elsewhere. Humanist political philosophy had established its own "discourse," sharing a set of themes, rhetorical strategies, and vocabulary. More exploits this discourse at the same time that he subjects it to a penetrating critique. In so doing, he transformed the conventional ideas of his predecessors in a way that invests his work with a stunning originality.

There are other influences on *Utopia*, apart from classical and humanist works, that are often overlooked. First among these are the satiric dialogues of the second-century Greek writer Lucian, some of which More had translated in collaboration with Erasmus.[7] Lucian's skepticism led him to imbue his dialogues with irony of every sort: comic, verbal, and structural. Much of the irony comes from the writer's use of naive narrating personae, and from the degree to which the dialogues are dramatized. Lucian's dialogues are much more fully dramatized than are those of Plato, showing a strong influence of Greek comic drama. More was impressed by all these elements, for they not only appealed to his propensity for joking and delight in dramatic play but also furnished useful tools for the presentation of his own ambivalent vision. He was also influenced by Lucian's *True History*, a fantasy voyage to a strange island where very peculiar things happen. In short, it is precisely the literary elements that More took from Lucian that turned *Utopia* from a conventional humanist treatise into the enigmatic fiction that has teased the imagination and challenged the interpretative power of men and women ever since.

The hints that More picked up from the fantastical voyage of Lucian were reinforced by information about some real voyages that seem to have excited More's imagination: Amerigo Vespucci's account of the four voyages he made to the New World and South America between 1497 and 1504. In *Utopia* More states that Hythlodaeus was Vespucci's constant companion during the last three of those four voyages (i.e., the ones to Brazil), "which are now universally read of" (51/7).[8] One should not underestimate the impact of Vespucci's travelogues on More. They gave a vivid description of a hitherto-unknown New World in which the Indians held all things in common; did not value gold, pearls, gems, or any of the other things considered precious in Europe; and, moreover, led a manner of living that Vespucci judged to be "Epicurean" (Vespucci, 97). Here, then, was an actual society that put flesh on the abstract ideals of Plato's *Republic* and seemed to materialize some of the moral values being preached by the Christian humanists. If Lucian had given More a literary form capable of presenting his vision in all its paradoxical ambivalence, Vespucci's account gave him a material form through which he could conceptualize it. All he had to do was fill Vespucci's paradigm with details according to his own insights and fancy. The idea of combining Lucian's manner with Vespucci's matter, and of filtering the whole through the lens of his own ambivalent vision, proved, for More, irresistible.

2

The Importance of the Work

Utopia is unquestionably one of the great works of original genius of all time. It initiated the form of social thought we know as "utopian idealism." With its realistic blueprint for a society that could serve as "a nursery of correct and useful institutions" for succeeding ages,[1] *Utopia* has been a source of inspiration for social reformers from the early sixteenth century until the present day, as witnessed by several attempts in the Americas to set up communities founded on the institutions outlined in that work.[2] It has been claimed, with some justice, that *Utopia* "did more to make William Morris a Socialist than ever Karl Marx did."[3]

Just as significantly, More's book inaugurated a literary genre to which it has given its name.[4] Several of the generic elements More used were not new. Fantasy voyages, such as Lucian's *True History*, had been written before, and Plato's *Republic* had provided the model for many later philosophical writings on the nature of the ideal state. More's innovation was to blend these two traditions together, introducing in the process a new degree of fictive realism. The genre More invented, now known as the literary utopia, may be defined as the representation of an ideal, nonexistent society as if it actually existed, usually under the fiction of a distant country that is at some remove from that of the author and reader. More's original exercise in this genre has been repeatedly imitated in works such as Francis Bacon's *New Atlantis* (1627), Edward Bellamy's *Looking Backward* (1888), William Morris's *News from Nowhere* (1891), and Aldous Huxley's *Island* (1962).

Utopia may also be viewed as the prototype of the obverse genre, the dystopia. The paradigm More created lends itself ideally to satire, because the distance between his imaginary society and the society in which he lived enabled him to contrast the two. Nevertheless, this paradigm allows satire to work in either direction, depending on whether the contrast between the imaginary and actual societies is favorable or unfavorable. Many writers after More have seized the possibility of creating an imaginary society in which disturbing tendencies in actual society are brought to a frightening culmination. When satire works *against* an imaginary society, the utopia turns into its opposite, the dystopia. Some striking examples are Huxley's *Brave New World* (1932), George Orwell's *Nineteen Eighty-four* (1949), Ursula LeGuin's *The Dispossessed: An Ambiguous Utopia* (1974), and Anthony Burgess's *A Clockwork Orange* (1962).

More's *Utopia* retains its power to fascinate and disturb because no one has yet been able to fix with certainty the relative extent of utopian and dystopian elements in the society it depicts. On the one hand, certain institutions in *Utopia* seem "progressive" in their equity and rationality, and therefore desirable; on the other, certain other practices seem repellent and to be rejected. Moreover, readers differ in their opinion as to which features are desirable and which are detestable. In short, the text itself seems riddled with ambiguities.

The reason for these ambiguities can readily be explained. The shape, form, and even vision of *Utopia* evolved by degrees, as More first grew uneasy with the fruits of his utopian speculations and then found himself confronted with the need to make a major career decision about which he felt extremely ambivalent. The outward consequences are to be seen in the way the traveler's account which constitutes book 2 is placed within a dramatized dialogue, which is further surrounded by prefatory letters by various real-life persons offering diverse opinions on the work itself. Furthermore, we are made to suspect that the traveler's tale in book 2 is offered by a narrator who is unreliable and whose account is enfolded within the narration of a second, equally unreliable narrator who is also reporting a colloquy between three people that he admits he may not have perfectly recalled. On top of all this, More ranges through every degree of tone from the purely facetious to the vehemently satiric. In this way, More deliberately conceals his personal belief and destabilizes the meaning of the work so that the identification of a single, determinate meaning becomes impossible.

It is precisely because the work evolved in this fashion that it ends up offering an extraordinarily profound comment on utopianism itself. The fact that More allowed the irony and paradoxes arising from his deepening ambivalence to remain fixed within the fabric of his invention turns the invention into a symbolic representation that fully captures the element of equivocal awareness at the very heart of the utopian impulse. More's awareness of this equivocal element is built into the brilliant pun of the work's title. "Utopia" is a compound of the Greek words *ou* (not) and *topos* (place); it can also be taken, however, as punning on *eu,* meaning "happy." The interchangeable prefix thus captures a fundamental paradox inherent in utopianism: the utopian vision is liable to contain the seeds of its own subversion in the form of doubts as to whether the "ideal" it proposes is attainable—or even desirable—given the realities of the human condition. It is remarkable that the very prototype of the utopian genre should so completely adumbrate all the problems inherent in the utopian vision itself. By creating a fiction that fully encompasses the paradoxical interrelationship between hope and doubt and optimism and pessimism, More made a major contribution to the intellectual heritage of the world.

There is one final reason for the importance of *Utopia.* By identifying the tensions in humanist utopianism, More showed prophetically why the Reformation would happen. In a situation where people looked to change their society radically through reforms based in moral idealism but were also led to doubt that these reforms could be achieved, people felt the need to seek a fuller explanation of life than the pious moral platitudes of humanism could provide—unless, of course, they simply were to agree with Machiavelli that men had to "learn how not to be virtuous" if they were to succeed in this world.[5] In particular, they sought to understand why the world should apparently be so dominated by the universal human sinfulness that seemed to hinder reform. The person who would offer a more compelling explanation was an Augustinian monk named Martin Luther. When Luther nailed his list of 95 theses to the door of a Roman Catholic church in Wittenberg, Germany, thunderously denouncing indulgences, Europe was set ablaze, and a religious revolution was unleashed that would rapidly supersede the humanists' reform effort, producing consequences they had hardly foreseen. *Utopia* shows that More was aware of the tensions that would provoke the Protestant Reformation and that he, long before anyone else, attempted to come to terms with them.

3

Critical Reception

Since it first issued from the Louvain press of Thierry Martens in late 1516, *Utopia* has received high acclaim for its imaginative brilliance and wisdom as an essay in social idealism. The enthusiasm it generates is just as evident in the comments of modern political historians as it was in those of More's humanist contemporaries. Moreover, this enthusiasm crosses ideological, cultural, and national boundaries (*Utopia* has been translated into almost every language of culture, including those as diverse as Chinese and Breton). The appeal of More's masterpiece can thus be judged to be timeless and universal.

Utopia has, nevertheless, generated more critical disagreement than any other literary text in the Western tradition. Commentators have been unable to agree on where its norms lie. Some have seen its values as conservative and medieval, with More looking backwards to the corporate life of Christian monasticism (Chambers, 136).[1] Others have seen it as a progressive window to the future because of the radicalism of its institutions.[2] Its philosophical assumptions have been identified variously as Platonic, Aristotelian, and Augustinian.[3] Interpretation is complicated still further by the fact that critical responses to *Utopia* have always divided sharply into those that take it to be a serious work of political philosophy and those that take it to be a speculative exercise written largely for entertainment.[4]

EARLY REACTIONS

The first readers of *Utopia*, the members of More's own humanist circle, were in no doubt: they took *Utopia* for the most part seriously, while participating in the joke fostered by the erudite puns inherent in the names within the work, and responded to it with wild enthusiasm. This is most evident in the prefatory epistles that More himself had Erasmus procure for the printed editions. Guillaume Budé, the foremost French humanist of the day, saw the *Utopian* commonwealth as embodying "the customs and the true wisdom of Christianity," and therefore believed that it furnished a "model of the happy life" (11/6–15, 13/16). Peter Giles, a young scholar from Antwerp, supplied a hexastichon (a poem of six metrical lines), claiming that *Utopia* surpassed Plato's *Republic* because it actually embodied the things Plato merely talked about (21/1–9). John Desmarais of Cassel, public rhetor at the University of Louvain, judged that "whatever pertains to the good constitution of a commonwealth may be seen in it as in a mirror" (27/34–36), and Jerome Busleyden, a famous jurist, also saw it as a "pattern and perfect model of morality, whose equal has never been seen anywhere in the world for the soundness of its constitution, for its perfection, and for its desirability," far surpassing the commonwealths of the Spartans, Athenians, and Romans (35/1–6). From these judgments it can be seen that More's contemporaries took *Utopia* as a serious model for reform; some of them, indeed, believed that the Utopian commonwealth actually existed, if we can believe More's own statement to Giles and the comment of Nicholas Harpsfield.[5]

The enthusiasm that *Utopia* first excited, however, was soon tempered by the controversy that began to surround More when he began to become a politically significant figure. This occurred as soon as he took sides in the Reformation dispute between the English Lutherans and adherents to Roman Catholicism. Reformers, like William Tyndale or John Frith, who had taken *Utopia* as evidence of an enlightened outlook in More, were dismayed when he declared his vehement opposition not only to their doctrinal views but also to their plans for the reform of church and state in England. They took this as evidence of inconsistency; after all, he had allowed his utopians to have married priests, divorce, and a social system that would eliminate the ostentatious materialism they saw afflicting the Church—precisely the things for which they were arguing. Their response was to either deride *Utopia* as "vain poetry" or use it as evidence that More had seen the truth but was hypocritically betraying it—as Tyndale sneeringly jibed—"for to get promotion."[6] By the time several decades had elapsed, many Protestants had come to regard *Utopia* merely as a piece of juggling sophistry, showing More's readiness to say anything for effect, without sincerity or integrity. John Foxe's attitude is typical: More writes, he argues, "by three or four mighty arguments, as big as mill-posts, fetched out of Utopia, from whence thou must know, reader, can come no fictions, but all fine poetry."[7]

An equally striking cooling off took place in the attitude of members on the opposing side. Once More had declared his commitment to Roman Catholic orthodoxy in the 1520s and 1530s, *Utopia* became an acute embarrassment, not least for the author himself. By the time More wrote *The Confutation of Tyndale's Answer* in 1532, he had come to regret the fact that he had ever written the earlier work; indeed, he wished it could be burnt.[8] Equally sensitive to the potentially damaging effect of *Utopia* on More's reputation were the Marian hagiographers who extolled More as a martyr during the reign of the Catholic Queen Mary I, and the recusants who sought to keep his reputation alive during the reign of Elizabeth I. William Roper, More's son-in-law, ignores *Utopia* completely in the anecdotal notes he provided for the "official" life of More. Nicholas Harpsfield, who wrote up the formal version, does mention *Utopia* but glides over all difficulties with the innocent statement that it describes "an excellent and absolute state of commonwealth . . . saving [that] the people were unchristian" (Roper and Harpsfield, 110). The Catholic editors of the 1565 Louvain edition of More's collected works in Latin were less coy: they actively censored *Utopia*, purging it of the anticlerical episode concerning the ignorant friar at the table of Cardinal John Morton.[9] That both sides in the Reformation controversy felt it necessary to regard *Utopia* with circumspection is significant in itself. It points to the fact that the work's quintessence is something that neither Protestant nor Catholic partisans understood, and that its meaning cannot be confined to either of their religious ideologies. Indeed, that is partly the reason for *Utopia's* continued universal appeal.

CONTINUITY OF THE EARLY APPROACHES

Within several decades, then, the main lines of approach to *Utopia* had been established: (a) that it is a serious political treatise representing More's own enlightened vision of a reformed society; (b) that it is proof of massive inconsistency—or, worse, hypocrisy—in him; and (c) that it is merely a fanciful intellectual exercise that does not represent More's real opinion. These views have persisted, with various permutations and modifications, to the present day.

The early humanists' view that *Utopia* is a work of serious political philosophy finds its equivalent in the opinions of modern scholars, who have approached the work from the standpoint of political theory or political, social, or economic history. Karl Kautsky, for example, made More a prophet of modern communism when he declared in the 1920s that More was one of the few who have been capable of making the bold intellectual leap, of seeing a "newly evolving mode of production," based on material conditions, together with the social consequences and "more rational mode of production" to which it would lead.[10] Others using the same serious approach have reached different conclusions. Russell Ames saw *Utopia* as "a product of capitalism's attack on feudalism, a part of middle-class and humanist criticism of a decaying social order."[11]

The weakness of all such readings is that they naively overlook the ironies and ambiguities in *Utopia*. As soon as its complexity started to be acknowledged, modifications had to be made to the notion of its seriousness. This occurred in the work of Dermot Fenlon, Quentin Skinner, and George Logan.[12] Their revisions hinge on the idea that the ironic complexities of *Utopia* show More to be presenting a humanist critique of humanism itself. Thus Skinner argues that the beliefs of "civic" or Ciceronian humanism are brought sharply into conflict with a Platonist outlook so as to present a challenge to More's fellow humanists to question the coherence of their own political thought.[13] In a similar vein, Logan argues that "More's aim is to fuse city-state theory with universal-state theory by reconciling Aristotle's empirical approach with the idealism of universal-state theory, and by bringing the analytic methods of city-state theory to bear on the problem of realizing Stoic and Christian ideals."[14] Many readers, I suspect, will find these modifications of the old view ingenious rather than convincing.

The view of the early Protestants, that *Utopia* attests to a fundamental inconsistency in More's political thinking, and the counter-view of the early Catholic hagiographers, that no inconsistency existed, likewise found plenty of later exponents. The Protestant view, in fact, came to dominate the assessment of More by English historians throughout the eighteenth and nineteenth centuries. It was formulated in its sharpest terms by Bishop Gilbert Burnet in his *History of the Reformation of the Church of England*, which held that More had "emancipated himself, and had got into a Scheme of free Thoughts" when he wrote *Utopia* but had later welshed on his humanism when he "came to muffle up his Understanding, and deliver himself up as a Property to the blind and enraged Fury of the Priests."[15] This view was reiterated, with varying degrees of severity, by later liberal historians, notably Frederic Seebohm (355–58).

In response to allegations that *Utopia* proves More's inconsistency, Catholic commentators have evolved various strategies for interpreting it so as to support the idea that he was consistent throughout his career. One tactic, first formulated by James Mackintosh and T. E. Bridgett,[16] is to regard it as a jeu d'esprit that, as C. S. Lewis puts it, should not be taken "*au grand sérieux*" (Lewis, 167). *Utopia*, says Lewis, "appears confused only so long as we are trying to get out of it what it never intended to give. It becomes intelligible and delightful as soon as we take it for what it is—a holiday work, a spontaneous overflow of intellectual high spirits, a revel of debate, paradox, comedy and (above all) of invention, which starts many hares and kills none." He concludes emphatically, "There is no inconsistency. More was from the first a very orthodox Papist" (Lewis, 170–71).

The other main strategy used by scholars to resolve the problem of More's consistency is to adopt Harpsfield's device for reading *Utopia*: that is, to see it as the most perfect state attainable by pagans who have reason alone to guide them. The chief exponent of this view was R. W. Chambers in his influential biography of More, who claims that "the underlying thought of *Utopia* always is, *With nothing save Reason to guide them, the Utopians do this; and yet we Christian Englishmen, we Christian Europeans . . . !*" (Chambers,

170–71). Later this view was elaborated by the Jesuit scholar Father Edward Surtz, one of the editors of the Yale edition of More's works, whose books remain the standard Roman Catholic interpretation of *Utopia.* In Surtz's argument, "More is far from setting up Utopia, the ideal republic of paganism, as the exemplar for Christian Europe." The Utopians possess revelation and religion that are only natural, not supernatural, and are therefore liable to error until they receive the advantage of the revealed verities of the Catholic Church. This, Surtz declares, is clearly the unambiguous message that the book is designed to teach, through a presentation that is neither wholly jesting nor wholly serious. Any wit or irony can be accounted for, Surtz says, by More's desire to make its teaching "delightful," as a means of imparting his orthodox message more effectively.[17]

By the 1970s these three main approaches to *Utopia*—that of the political theorists, the Protestant, and the Catholic—had presented critics with a conundrum: all of them could not be right, yet the persistence of each suggested that there were some grounds to justify all. The challenge for the next period of criticism was to find out how this could be so.

CONTEMPORARY CRITICISM

All the readings described so far are, to varying degrees, manifestly partial misreadings because their assumptions are too simple to account for the aspects of *Utopia* that give rise to the other interpretations that contradict them. In particular, they fail to convincingly explain the complexities of the work because they overlook them altogether, try to resolve them at too crude a level, or, at the other extreme, offer synthetic solutions that defy credibility. Most readers are likely to feel that none of the traditional interpretations fully matches up with their own experience of the text.

Astonishing developments in modern critical theory since the 1970s may change all that. New critical approaches have begun to emerge that can more adequately recognize and explain the literary and intellectual complexity of *Utopia.* Modern theory has established that the relationships of a text to its author, readers, and

world are much more intricate and subtle than earlier commentators supposed, particularly in the case of a text like More's,
which makes no pretense at offering a "closed" meaning determined
and controlled by the author. The lines of connection are often indi-
rect, involving symbolic displacement or other means of self-repre-
sentation. Conventions carry with them their own inherited meaning with which the author negotiates as he or she creates each new
text. On the other side, part of the meaning of a text resides in the
responses that it elicits from readers, and those responses are
subject to a range of variability that widens the more open, or dia-
logic, a text is. Awareness of such issues has produced a whole set
of new perspectives on *Utopia* in criticism since the mid-1960s.

In the 1960s scholars became increasingly dissatisfied with the
smoothness with which critics of the hagiographical school,
whether of the Roman Catholic or Protestant variety, ironed out all
the interpretative difficulties that most readers feel they encounter
when they try to make sense of *Utopia*. A new awareness began to
emerge that *Utopia* is constructed as an ironic representation
rather than a straightforward narrative, in a long line of such ironic
works that appeared during the English Renaissance.[18] One critic
went so far as to argue that *Utopia* is, in fact, a dystopia.[19] By
paying much more attention to its rhetorical structure and status
as a fiction, critics began to recognize that the work is calculatedly
ambiguous, and that if "Utopia" could exist anywhere, it was less a
final goal than a stance or state of mind.[20] (Unfortunately, this
advance in critical understanding did not find its way into either of
the contributions of the two editors of the Yale edition of *Utopia*.)

The increased sensitivity of scholars in the 1970s and 1980s to
the nature and function of More's rhetorical strategies has yielded
some of the most illuminating theories to date. Dermot Fenlon's
proposal that *Utopia* offers a critique of the humanist reform program itself has been taken up enthusiastically by such scholars as
Quentin Skinner, although Skinner has recently modified his earlier views. Joel Altman's study of the effects of formal grammar-
school training in rhetoric on early Tudor drama enabled him to
detect in *Utopia* the presence of a mind conditioned to argue "*in
utramque partem*"—on both sides of the question. Grammar-school
training, he argues equipped authors with a number of specific
rhetorical forms, gave them a predilection for debate, and accus-

tomed them to using disconcerting shifts of viewpoint as a means of examining the many sides of a given theme. Armed with these perceptions, he was able to see that More's addition of a dialogue to the original essay in social idealism drastically changed the work's shape by mingling the different expectations of contrary rhetorical forms: "The completed piece now became an ambivalent anecdote comprising an introductory narration, an ethopoetic dialogue (furnished with conventional garden setting) and extended argument via exemplum, and a qualifying palinode. It was a form through which More was confronting the challenge of his own vision."[21] Altman's analysis convincingly consolidated suggestions made earlier by R. S. Sylvester.[22]

The attention that has been devoted in recent years to the ironic literary techniques More used in *Utopia* has resulted in a fairly widespread consensus that the work has none of the definitiveness of meaning that earlier interpreters proposed. This remains true even in the face of the advent of postmodern theories of critical interpretation. Investigating *Utopia* in the light of contemporary hermeneutics and reader-response theory, for example, Elizabeth McCutcheon reaches conclusions similar to those of W. J. Barnes, Robbin S. Johnson, and other commentators from the 1960s. Her 1983 study analyzes More's prefatory letter addressed to Peter Giles to show how it serves as a poetics and hermeneutics for *Utopia*. This letter, she argues, is concerned with the aesthetics of honest deception that underpins *Utopia* and that is designed to exercise the reader's mind, imagination, and moral sense. This aesthetics prepares the reader for experiencing the work itself, by presenting ambiguities and fictions that adumbrate the formal paradoxes of the larger work. *Utopia*, in McCutcheon's view, is pervasively paradoxical by design. Paradox, she declares, "enabled [More] to evoke rather than to explain ideas, values, and attitudes, to explore problems nonsystematically and wittily, wholly to involve his readers, startling them into a search for truth and insisting upon some reaction (since otherwise a paradox is not really completed). It enabled him to be engaged and disengaged, seriously playful and playfully philosophical at once, shifting modes and moods at will."[23]

Both Altman's and McCutcheon's treatments escape from the limitations of earlier views that saw *Utopia* either as wholly serious or simply as a jeu d'esprit. They avoid, too, the assumption that More's viewpoint must have been definitively one thing or another by substituting the process that the text induces for the idea of a fixed, determinate meaning. In so doing, they affirm the most essential and distinctive features of *Utopia* as a work of fiction.

Rhetorical, hermeneutical, and reader-response theories have helped critics to establish how More wrote *Utopia*, but not why. For that, one must turn to the studies of those who have attempted to relate the work to More's own personality via modern psychoanalytic criticism. One such attempt is that of Stephen Greenblatt, who sees *Utopia* as central to "the complex interplay in More's life and writings of self-fashioning and self-cancellation, the crafting of a public role and the profound desire to escape from the identity so crafted."[24] Recognizing that "*Utopia* presents two distinct worlds that occupy the same textual space while insisting upon the impossibility of their doing so," Greenblatt accounts for this by arguing that Hythlodaeus represents all that More deliberately excluded from the personality he created and played: "he is the sign of More's awareness of his own self-creation, hence his own incompleteness." In this reading, *Utopia* is seen as an exercise in profound self-criticism in which More allows his public self and his excluded self to fight it out. Utopia's institutions are designed to reduce the size of the ego, and hence the book functions as a strategy of self-cancellation. In this way, Greenblatt argues, More was seeking to assuage guilt at possibly having distanced himself from God by adopting the life he had chosen for himself (Greenblatt, 22–58).

Greenblatt's interpretation, too, breaks out of the mold of conventional approaches to *Utopia*, but many readers will find the model of identity formation on which this interpretation is predicated too clumsy as a device for fully explaining why More wrote the book. There is a much greater range of tone, of approval and disapprobation, of exhilaration and melancholy, in *Utopia* than the theory can account for.

If this brief, and very selective, survey of the critical reception of *Utopia* has shown one thing above others, it is that the book is so variegated and comprehensive as to make all attempts at interpretation perilous and liable to seem reductive. The problem is that More's own range of intellectual, psychological, and emotional responses to his material, as represented within the work itself, was so great as already to encompass almost every kind of reaction that the book is likely to excite. The various types of interpretation that have been traced in this chapter are, in many cases, radically at odds with one another precisely because readers have responded only to a limited number of aspects of the work that, because of ideological or political affiliations, they are predisposed to see. Inevitably, partial and partisan readings have been produced as a result. None of these can be totally dismissed, for they were made possible in the first place by More's range of responses to his imaginative vision. Students and scholars of *Utopia* need to find an interpretative framework able to accommodate the widest possible range of critical reactions. Which one to choose must remain a matter for the individual, according to his or her reading experience; it is sufficiently capacious to sustain all.

A READING

❖

The title page of the third edition of *Utopia*, printed in Basel by
Johannes Froben in March 1518. *The Bodleian Library, Oxford*

4

Approaching *Utopia*

Readers' initial reaction to *Utopia* is likely to be a mixture of excitement, perplexity, frustration, and despair: excitement at how enlightened and sensible many aspects of Utopian polity are, perplexity at the presence of other features that seem either repellent or absurd, frustration at the impossibility of locating any stable ground from which to view the work, and despair at the prospect of trying to make critical sense of the whole. Scholars of the past tried to solve the problem simply by forcing *Utopia* to conform to their own preferred interpretative paradigms, viewing the text as (a) a straightforward exposition of political philosophy of which More wholly approved, (b) a pagan philosophical state lacking Christian revelation of which he disapproved, (c) a mere joke written for entertainment's sake, or (d) a harshly satiric dystopia. All such paradigms tend to derive from models too simple to accommodate the full range of evidence in *Utopia*. These interpretations demand that all nonconforming details be suppressed, which has resulted in a number of mutually contradictory readings, all of which accurately identify certain aspects of *Utopia* but ultimately distort to a greater or lesser extent.

The breakthrough for students of *Utopia* occurs when they recognize that the confused reaction they have to it is the product of More's rhetorical design, which is itself contrived to induce precisely that effect. Part of *Utopia*'s meaning, in fact, resides in the speculative dialogue that More anticipates readers will carry on indefinitely after they have finished reading the book. Nevertheless, students of *Utopia* still need to be able to account for why and how the work functions as such, and for this reason I am going to describe two different approaches to *Utopia*: one that takes the work "as is," and one that follows the chronological order of its composition rather than its final rhetorical order. The first approach explains why students react to *Utopia* in the almost universal way they do; the second explains how it was that More wrote the work to have this effect.

READING *UTOPIA* AS IT WAS FIRST PUBLISHED

The first readers of *Utopia* were confronted with a small book bearing a remarkable resemblance to Martin Waldseemüller's *Cosmographiae introductio*, in which were printed the *Four Voyages of Amerigo Vespucci* that More mentions as being "universally read of" (51/7). It had similar physical dimensions, being a quarto measuring 7.75 by 5 inches. It also had its share of prefatory verses and letters, woodcut illustrations, and subject subheadings, just as Waldseemüller's text did, except that those in *Utopia* were even more elaborate. Also, it purported to give an account of "the new island of Utopia," just as Waldseemüller's title page had declared that *Cosmographiae introductio* would touch on "lands which were unknown to Ptolemy, and have been recently discovered" (Vespucci, 31). In outward appearance, then, *Utopia* was designed to arouse expectations that it would be yet another account of the discoveries being made. To this extent, its physical form was designed to complement its author's attempts at literary verisimilitude. The purpose of both was to elicit credibility.

On proceeding through the parerga (prefatory matter), readers would have seen their initial expectations confirmed by the panoply of actual "evidence" (the woodcut showing the city of Amaurotum, followed by the Utopian alphabet and a specimen of poetry written in the Utopian vernacular). The excited reactions of Peter Giles (in his letter to Jerome Busleyden), John Desmarais of Cassel (in his letter to Giles and poem on Utopia), and Busleyden (in his letter to More) would then have primed them to expect that, as the title page and the poem in the Utopian vernacular had already claimed, the description of this newly discovered island would also present them with "that ideal of a commonwealth, that pattern and perfect model of morality, whose equal has never been seen anywhere in the world for the soundness of its constitution, for its perfection, and for its desirability" (35/1–4). Finally, More's own prefatory letter, with its request for Giles to corroborate certain details, would have further lulled the unsuspecting reader to believe that this was going to be the true account of an actual place.

My point is this: up to the moment when More's own narrative begins, everything about *Utopia* has predisposed the reader to read the text as if it were (a) an actual place and (b) the model of an ideal commonwealth, with the actuality of the place serving to enhance its credibility. When, however, the narrative gets under way, it is not long before a dispute develops that puts the status of the Utopian model, and the worth of even contemplating it, in doubt. Hythlodaeus, the Portuguese philosopher-traveler who has been to Utopia, and "More," the character who recounts his story, fall into a violent disagreement as to whether a wise man should enter the service of a king. Hythlodaeus believes it is pointless: on the one hand, rulers will not listen to good advice; on the other, it is impossible to achieve any lasting reforms as long as private property—the root of pride, and hence of all evils—exists. "More," to the contrary, believes that every good man is obliged to offer advice to rulers, and that even those things that cannot be made perfectly good are capable of being made as little bad as possible, as long as the wise man is prepared to act obliquely, adapting his behavior to suit the play at hand. In short, Hythlodaeus is not prepared to settle for anything but the best, because he believes the best state of a commonwealth can, and has been, attained (in Utopia), whereas "More" remains skeptical at this possibility and is prepared to accommodate himself to what he takes to be the inevitability of human imperfection.

The presence of this dispute in book 1 instantly undermines reader expectations that the title page and parerga have aroused—the idea that the Utopian commonwealth will furnish an ideal model—without negating these expectations entirely. If, as "More" claims, human nature is inherently and irremediably evil, then no society could ever be devised whose institutions would not be tainted by it. Hythlodaeus's refusal to concur with More's pessimistic viewpoint, however, keeps alive the possibility that the just society can indeed be attained once the root causes of social injustice—private wealth and the cash economy—are eradicated. The burden of proof is made to rest with the description of Utopia itself in book 2, which Hythlodaeus confidently anticipates will confirm his point of view. Thus by the end of book 1, the reader's interpretative bearings have been deliberately confused. The book's form and parerga have earlier aroused one set of expectations that the dialogue in book 1 progressively threatens to unsettle, until the promise of a conclusive exemplum seems to open up the way again for renewed hope.

This process continues and intensifies in book 2, which, in terms of the deliberate balancing of optimistic expectations with skeptical and pessimistic reservations, repeats the pattern of book 1, but in a still more unsettling way. The rationality of Utopian institutions at first seems to confirm Hythlodaeus's point of view, but then elements of comic irony and satire begin to obtrude until, at one point (in the description of their war practices), the Utopians seem to be even more fiendishly evil than Europeans. Hythlodaeus's concluding eulogy of Utopia as the just society invites us to regard it in a way that the representation itself has made impossible, because of the ironies depicted in the account that Hythlodaeus himself seems incapable of seeing. Our reluctance to have complete confidence in Hythlodaeus as a narrator is finally reinforced by the mixed reaction expressed by "More," who remains unconvinced, but not absolutely so. The final effect of *Utopia*, when read in the form in which it was first published, is to leave readers suspended in a state of equivocation—caught between the desire to believe Hythlodaeus and the inability to ignore the reservations of "More."

READING *UTOPIA* ACCORDING TO ITS COMPOSITION SEQUENCE

The key to understanding the ambiguous nature of *Utopia* is provided by a crucial remark made by Erasmus. In his famous description of More sent to Ulrich von Hutten in 1519, Erasmus declares that More "had written the second book [of *Utopia*] at his leisure, and afterwards, when he found it was required, added the first off-hand."[1] On the basis of this information, we can suppose that the account of Utopia was written sometime between July and October 1515, when More was killing time in the Netherlands, waiting for diplomatic negotiations to resume, and that book 1 was composed sometime between November 1515 and August 1516, after he had returned to London.[2]

An illuminating pattern begins to emerge if we read the work in this order. Book 2 begins as a relatively straightforward narrative account of Utopia, describing the island's geography, cities, population distribution, agricultural practices, method of government, and streets, houses, and gardens. There is almost nothing at this stage to suggest that the account is anything other than the kind of neutral, factual description that Vespucci supplies of the new lands he discovered. The absence of pervasive ironic subversion in this opening section leads us to suspect that when More began to entertain himself in Bruges by inventing an imaginary society he did so by creating it as a genuine *eutopia* (happy place)—a society constructed ideally according to all the rational and moral principles he held most dear.

It is only when he moves on to describing Utopians' social relations that tensions begin to appear in the narrative. Most readers feel varying degrees of discomfort with certain Utopian practices, such as Utopians' attitude toward colonialism and the ways in which they regulate the conduct of their citizens. This discomfort increases as More proceeds to describe their pleasure ethic (with the euthanasia and marriage practices it appears to promote) and Utopian war practices, which involve bribery, assassination, the hiring of mercenaries, and the subversion of neighboring realms through covert fifth-columnist activities. The narrative of book 2 progressively appears to lose confidence in those aspects of life that give human nature scope to escape from regulation and restraint, so that by the end of the section on Utopian warfare the book seems to be in the process of turning itself into a fully fledged dystopia.

The balance between dystopian and eutopian elements only begins to be restored when More moves on to describe Utopian religion, and the realm of experience in which the human impulses shown elsewhere in book 2 come under the corrective guidance of religious faith. As far as their religious practices are concerned, the Utopians reveal a very different attitude compared with that which motivates some of their rationalistic social and political practices: they are far less dogmatic, far less absolutist, more tolerant, and more open to the possibility that divine providence may lead them in directions that their rational philosophy does not anticipate. In short, they are incipient ideal Christians in all but name, as their receptivity to the Gospel verifies. It is almost as if More, having come close to abandoning his vision of an ideal state, is trying to find some way of reclaiming it—at least partially.

Some critics may prefer to believe that More from the outset intended for his imaginary commonwealth to be a farrago of high seriousness, comedy, and satire, blending eutopian and dystopian elements together so as to create a witty and energizing paradox, but I doubt it. The pattern to be traced in book 2 is too marked and not susceptible to a more convincing explanation than the one I have given.

Even more compelling evidence that More experienced a loss of faith in his utopian vision in the course of creating it can be found in what he did to book 1, the part that was added after he returned to London. Everything to do with book 1 is designed to interpose rhetorical distance between More, the real-life author, and the imaginary society he created in book 2. First, his adding a dramatized dialogue to a straightforward narrative discourse in itself fundamentally changed the rhetorical status of book 2. It was now part of a larger fiction, the report of one narrator being reported within the report of another. Such a device made it far less likely that the descriptive account of Utopia in book 2 could be taken as directly representing the opinion of the real-life author by any but the most naïve of readers. Second, More's development of dramatic characters further enhanced this distance between himself and his creation. By inventing Hythlodaeus to be the narrator of book 2, More turned the narrator into merely one character among a number of others who exist in an ambiguous relationship with their author. In fact, by generating an argument between Hythlodaeus and a character named "More" that is never resolved conclusively, More opened up a further ambiguity: Which of the two narrators, if either, is to be trusted as reliable? On the one hand, it is possible to view "More" as merely a naïve stooge, set up as a rhetorical foil to throw Hythlodaeus's superior wisdom and integrity into greater relief; on the other, it is tempting to take him as a surrogate for the real More, given his seemingly sensible and persuasive plea for pragmatism and the politics of accommodation.

The same ambiguity surrounds Hythlodaeus as a narrator. His credibility is diminished by his failure to persuade the reader to share his interpretation of some of the experiences he reports—for example, the Morton episode in book 1 and, not least, his general perception of Utopia itself. It is further diminished by the way "More" tends to patronize him. And yet Hythlodaeus is never satisfactorily refuted—neither in his indignant rejection of the politics of accommodation as tainted and tainting nor in his concluding assertion that the Utopian commonwealth is "not merely the best but the only one which can rightly claim the name of a commonwealth" (237/38–39). In the way he devised book 1, then, More went to considerable lengths to disguise any personal affinity he may originally have felt with the imaginary society he had devised in book 2.

Why should this have been so? With the advantage of hindsight, we can see that More on his return to England from his utopian embassy was faced with the need to resolve an acute crisis in his personal life, and that the form of *Utopia* evolved in response to his complicated feelings concerning it. No sooner had More returned to London when Henry VIII offered him as annuity if he would enter the royal service. His perplexity is easy to imagine. Like other humanists, he had believed that the remedy for European ills lay in the reform of institutions according to the rational and ethical principles humanism had derived from the ancient pagans. Yet his recent attempt to imagine an actual society founded on these very principles had led him to conclude that human nature would always render the complete reform of society impossible. Here he was, then, faced with the offer of a position that would give him the opportunity—which all humanists hypothetically treasured—to promote humanistic reform by offering wise counsel to the prince. The problem for More was that he was being offered the chance to work toward a goal that his own imagination had shown him to be an illusion: no matter how rationally or philosophically a state was ordered, human nature would perpetuate the existence of sin and injustice, whether private wealth was abolished or not—that is what the ironies of his Utopian *exemplum* had uncovered.

What, then, was the point of giving up a highly lucrative and well-regarded position as a lawyer in the City of London (by the time he entered royal service More was earning about £400 per annum, far more than his annuity was worth) when he realized very well that his ability to influence affairs in any significant way was liable to prove futile? This was one reason that More wavered for over a year before making his decision. Despite his deepening skepticism about the reformist ideals and aspirations of his humanist peers, however, More could not quite prevent himself from continuing to share them. All through his life More experienced competing, and even contradictory, impulses, and he also possessed the unusual kind of consciousness that can encompass simultaneous and conflicting emotions, aspirations, and insights. It is therefore unsurprising that these aspects of his mind and personality should have manifested themselves in the fabric of his evolving fiction, especially given the pressure he was under to make an intellectual decision that would affect his future career.

Quite naturally, More developed *Utopia* into an instrument through which he could explore his dilemma in order to work out a response to it and, in the process, lead readers into experiencing the same condition of perception. This being so, it is little wonder that *Utopia* turned into a fiction of extraordinary, perhaps unparalleled, literary complexity, with irony, paradoxes, tonal shifts, and dramatized indirection all calculated to arouse interpretative uncertainty in the reader while ensuring that More's personal attitude remains carefully concealed.

As if More had not complicated the interpretation of *Utopia* enough with the addition of book 1, he allowed it to be further problematized by the treatment his finished *libellus* ("little book") received from its successive editors. The responsibility for seeing the first edition of *Utopia* through the press was given to Peter Giles, whose friendship and company More had shared during his stay in Antwerp, and Erasmus. More must have fully primed his two friends as to how he wanted *Utopia* published. In the letter he sent to Erasmus on 3 September 1516 accompanying the finished manuscript, apart from alerting Erasmus to the fact that he has added a prefatory letter to Giles, More feels no need to give any further explicit instructions: "I know from experience that I do not have to tell you to give proper attention to everything else."[3] Among the other things to which Erasmus paid "proper attention" were the inclusion of an engraving showing the island of Utopia, a sample of the Utopian alphabet, a poem in the Utopian vernacular supplied by Peter Giles that praises Utopia as "the philosophical city," and a number of marginal annotations written in collaboration with Giles to guide the reader.[4]

A couple of weeks later More again wrote to Erasmus, this time requesting *Utopia* to be "handsomely set off with the highest of rec-ommendations, if possible, from . . . both intellectuals and distin-guished statesmen" (*Letters*, no. 7, 76). Whether Erasmus and Giles knew it, More was setting them up. Ostensibly, as far as they would have been aware, he was inviting them to share complicity in the pretense that Utopia was a real place. But More had a deeper pur-pose. He was also giving them the chance to respond to his inven-tion as if it was the model of an ideal commonwealth, which is precisely how the parerga they procured and the marginal annota-tions depict it. In this way, given than More had already worked into the representation ironic dystopian elements that the responses of Erasmus and Giles appear not to acknowledge, he was allowing them, and the other humanists who contributed recom-mendations to the volume, to betray the fact that they, like Hythlo-daeus, were predisposed not to see in the work all that More had made sure there was to see.

The book as finally published thus works the efforts of Eras-mus and Giles into the fiction itself for the purpose of establishing an implicit analogy between them as editors and Hythlodaeus and "More" as narrators: they, too, are victims of the limitations of selective, subjective vision. The point More is implicitly allowing to be made is this: If these two respond in this way, what hope is there of ever escaping from the inherent limitations of human vision, in the way that the reformist idealism of contemporary humanists presupposed could be done? The response of his peers thus becomes yet another irony to expand the compounding ironies of the whole. A further effect of these parerga, as mentioned earlier, is to sustain the balance that More has set up between competing optimistic and pessimistic expectations. More specifically placed the optimistic parerga that affirm Utopia as the ideal philosophical

Desiderius Erasmus, by Quentin Massys, 1517. *Galleria Nazionale d'Arte
Antica in Palazzo Barberini, Rome.* Half of the diptych (with *Peter Giles,
facing page*) sent to More by his friends on the Continent to
commemorate his "Utopian" embassy.

Peter Giles (Petrus Aegidius), by Quentin Massys, 1517. *The Courtauld Institute of Art, University of London*

city immediately before the dialogue of book 1—which questions whether such an ideal is really attainable—to condition readers to the oscillation between positive and negative responses they will experience when encountering the description of Utopia proper.

More made one final effort to unsettle the interpretative complacency of his readers, by supplying his own preface for inclusion in the parerga to *Utopia.* As Elizabeth McCutcheon has convincingly shown, More's letter to Peter Giles serves to alert the reader that "an aesthetics of honest deception" will govern the presentation of Utopia, for the letter contains the same kinds of contradictions and ambiguities that are encountered in the larger work itself (McCutcheon, 5). It also anticipates the full range of responses that those contradictions and ambiguities will elicit from readers, according to whether they are "peevish," "ungrateful" in their dispositions, "wrongheaded" in their judgments, or "pleasantly and blithely [indulgent of] their inclinations" (43/30–35)—like most commentators invariably have done ever since the book first appeared.

I hope by now that the advantage of studying *Utopia* according to the order of its composition and compilation has become plain. If not a way of solving the conundrum, it is at least a way of understanding why one exists. It also helps to explain why More's *Utopia* remains the archetype of all utopias. Because of the way it captures More's developing ambivalence, together with how it integrates the contradictory responses of More's early readers into the representation itself, *Utopia* has already encompassed the full range of reactions any other utopia or dystopia would ever be able to depict. For this reason it is the epitome of utopianism itself.

5

"O Sacred Society!":
The Eutopia within Book 2

The fantasy commonwealth on which More exercised his imagination while at leisure in the Netherlands falls into three distinct sections. The first consists of a description of the economic and political arrangements of *Utopia*. The second consists of an account of the ethical principles of the Utopians and various attempts to apply them in the sphere of social relations. The third consists of a description of religious beliefs and practices in Utopia. Most striking about this division are the tonal shifts that mark the transition from one section to another and that prevail within each section generally. As I have argued, these shifts in tone may give us the essential clue to More's thinking during his composition of *Utopia*. They suggest that initial enthusiasm for his ideal society soon gave way to an ambivalence that had been latent from the outset, as More's imagination registered that almost every positive feature of his commonwealth simultaneously carried with it—at least potentially—an obverse element that was either negative or absurd. As this occurred he was faced with the prospect of either allowing his fiction to collapse entirely into a dystopian spoof or discovering some way that his skeptical findings could be incorporated into a larger vision that would show them, paradoxically, as supporting a positive outlook. As the tripartite structure of book 2 shows, he chose the latter course.

IDEAL ASPECTS OF THE COMMONWEALTH

The first section of book 2, describing the geography of Utopia, together with its economic and political arrangements, forms a *eutopia*—or "happy land," as Peter Giles called it in the prefatory hexastichon he gave Anemolius—all its own. More signals as much to the reader in various ways. In tone, this section is predominantly positive in a way that seems designed to encourage approval—apart from several undercurrents of irony that, as I will show, signal the onset of the more extensive ironic subversion that will pervade the book's second section. More's account of the Utopian economic and political system also ends with its own approving miniperoration:

> Now you can see how nowhere in there any license to waste time, nowhere any pretext to evade work—no wine shop, no alehouse, no brothel anywhere, no opportunity for corruption, no lurking hole, no secret meeting place. On the contrary, being under the eyes of all, people are bound either to be performing the usual labor or to be enjoying their leisure in a fashion not without decency. This universal behavior must of necessity lead to an abundance of all commodities. Since the latter are distributed evenly among all, it follows, of course, that no one can be reduced to poverty or beggary. (147/21–32)

Rhetorically, with its direct address to the reader, its accumulation of phrases in series, its repetitions, and its artfully contrived parallelisms, this eulogy prefigures the final eulogy of Utopia that Hythlodaeus will give in his concluding peroration to the whole work. It is almost as if More at the close of this first section has said most of what was closest to his heart about the best state he could imagine, and was tempted to end the work at this point.

The glossator, too (either Erasmus or Giles—it is uncertain which), responds enthusiastically to the eutopian elements in this opening section. In the margin next to More's preliminary eulogy, he pens ecstatically the most enthusiastic gloss in the work: "O Holy Commonwealth—and to be imitated even by Christians!" (*O sanctam rempublicam, & uel Christianis imitandem*). Such signals, on the part of both author and glossator, leave little room for readers to doubt how they are to respond to the Utopian model up to this point, and experience in the classroom has shown that few do. This is the section of *Utopia* that perennially excites those interested in the history of political thought or are themselves motivated by political or social idealism.

What, then, is it about More's eutopia that may have appealed to its creator, and which has continued to appeal to readers of *Utopia* to the present day? In the first place, Utopia is depicted symbolically, in this first section, in terms that condition the reader to respond to it as a positive place. This is evident in its very geographical appearance. The island is described as being "like a new moon" (*in lunae speciem renascentis*) with two horns that gradually taper round to form a crescent until they are only eleven miles across, as if they are completing a circle (111/7–13). It is a small detail, but one that creates a highly symbolic emblem. Utopia is "renascent": it is being born again, and is growing. In the Renaissance the new moon was also often used as a symbol of grace, while the circle was a symbol of perfection. The image is therefore full of hope, suggesting the creative, positive aspects of a society in a state of near perfection that the reader will encounter.

Other details help to enhance this positive feeling. Surrounded by the land that forms the horns of the crescent, the broad bay in the center of the island is "protected from the wind" (*prohibitis uentis*), so that it is calm like a lake rather than rough (111/14–15). The harbor is thus, as the marginal gloss recognizes, "a naturally safe place" (*Locus natura tutus*), as is the island itself, being separated from the adjoining mainland by a protective, 15-mile-wide channel that was excavated at the order of King Utopus (113/8–11). All these geographical details combine to invest Utopia with a reassuring ambiance of vitality on the one hand and security on the other.

More strengthens our awareness of the vitality of Utopia by giving the Utopians an imaginary history. Their long-standing responsiveness to historical possibilities for creative change has made them into a dynamic, progressive, evolving society rather than a static one. We are constantly reminded of the technological and cultural advances that the Utopians have made since they were first conquered by King Utopus, "who brought the rude and rustic people to such a perfection of culture and humanity as makes them now superior to almost all other mortals" (113/5–7). Utopus set up a basic social, political, and religious structure that it was left to posterity to "adorn and improve." During the 1,760 years of their recorded history the Utopians have constantly striven to achieve such adornment and improvements, which can be seen in the houses in which they live:

> At first the houses were low, mere cabins and huts, haphazardly made with any wood to hand, with mud-plastered walls. They had thatched the steeply sloping roofs with straw. But now all the homes are of handsome appearance with three stories. The exposed faces of the walls are made of stone or cement or brick, rubble being used as filling for the empty space between the walls. The roofs are flat and covered with a kind of cement which is cheap but so well mixed that it is impervious to fire and superior to lead in defying the damage caused by storms. They keep the winds out of their windows by glass (which is in very common use in Utopia) or sometimes by thin linen smeared with translucent oil or amber. (121/31 – 123/5)

Time and again, we get confirmation that the Utopian attitude is one that promotes material progress, among other things.

The advantages of this attitude are seen again in their quickness to exploit emergent opportunities presented to them by chance (or, as the Utopians would have it, providence). Twelve hundred years earlier, Hythlodaeus tells us, some Romans and Egyptians were shipwrecked on the island:

> Now mark what good advantage their industry took of this one opportunity. The Roman empire possessed no art capable of any use which they did not either learn from the shipwrecked strangers or discover for themselves after receiving the hints for investigation—so great a gain was it to them that on a single occasion some persons were carried to their shores from ours. (109/6–11)

Similarly, as we learn later in book 2, the Utopians eagerly appropriate the European art of printing and the manufacture of paper (183/28 – 185/2) and are highly receptive to Christianity when they hear about Christ's teaching, character, and miracles and the no less wonderful constancy of His many martyrs (217/36 – 219/10). In all these instances the Utopians are not merely passive recipients of new knowledge; they actively develop and extend it, so that their society, and even their beliefs, are constantly evolving.

Even their language is shown to be in a state of dynamic evolution. There are an extraordinary number of references in *Utopia* to words and names formerly used in their ancient language but that have now been replaced by newer ones. Utopia itself used to be called "Abraxa" (113/5); "phylarchs" used to be called "syphogrants" (123/9); the prince of each city used to be called "Barzanes" but in the modern tongue is known as "Ademus" (133/8–9). These changes all serve to reinforce the impression that Utopia is in a constant state of evolution that opens up its society to the greatest conceivable range of creative possibilities.

Through the use of such symbolic details as these More predisposes the reader subliminally to regard Utopia in a positive light. The actual description of Utopian social and political arrangements seems designed to satisfy these positive expectations. As various commentators have explained, the Utopian commonwealth incorporates the best social and political features of earlier classical prototypes, particularly Plato's *Republic* and *Laws*, and depends heavily on the Greek conception of the *polis*, or city-state, as consisting of "a system of reciprocally-affecting parts" (Logan, 132). This is acknowledged by the glossator himself when he comments on the lack of private property in Utopia and such features as the folding doors of their houses, which give admission to anyone, or the Utopians' practice of exchanging houses every 10 years by lot: "These features smack of Plato's community" (121/13). Accordingly, the Utopian commonwealth seems ideally equitable and rational in its demographic planning, its distribution of goods, and its political, judicial, and administrative systems.

Operating on an assumption that "likeness begets harmony," the Utopians have planned their cities to be "identical in language, traditions, customs, and laws . . . similar in layout and . . . similar even in appearance" (113/19–23 and passim). Extending this principle, they have ensured not only an even distribution of cities but also of houses through the countryside and of the population generally. In this way they have eliminated the kind of rivalry between cities that could lead any one to desire to extend its borders at the expense of another.

Moreover, by implementing a system of common ownership, they have achieved the same harmony in social relations as they have in civic relations. A system of collective labor and planned food production has made it possible for all members of the population to have a plentiful supply of necessary things, so that no one is tempted to demand an excessive amount (139/1–5). Because the absence of private possessions has rendered pointless the ostentatious display of personal wealth, not only avarice and greed but also pride have been dramatically diminished.

Apart from these most fundamental institutions, other practices of the Utopians display a comparable rationality and apparent enlightenment. Their concern that all citizens should enjoy sensible working loads and conditions seems ahead of its time (127/25–37), as does their conception of the dignity of labor (e.g., 113/13), which has been described as "a milestone in the history of utopian thought" (Manuel and Manuel, 127). Equally impressive are the provisions they make for sanitary conditions in their cities, attractive street plans incorporating public gardens, hospitals, and even a town water supply (121/1–25, 139/15– 141/11).

Perhaps most impressive of all are the enlightened features of their political and judicial systems. The Utopians enjoy a fully democratic system of ascending power, administered through a form of conciliar government. They ensure that political decisions are of the highest quality by invoking a rule that no matter may be debated on the same day on which it is first proposed, that no decision on a matter of public business can be ratified unless it has been discussed in the senate on three separate days. They guard against tyranny by banning debate on public business outside the senate or the popular assembly, thus inhibiting the kind of conspiracies that could lead to it. They also ensure that the order of the commonwealth is not changed, by annually rotating elected office holders, and by including representatives from household groups as observers at each senate meeting (123/8– 125/24). As far as their legal system is concerned, we are told later in book 2 that they have reduced the opportunities for corruption by making very few laws and by ensuring that these laws are simple enough to allow individual citizens to conduct their own cases (195/8–39).

More takes care to impress on the reader that the Utopian socioeconomic system is not merely rationally desirable from the viewpoint of equity but also has many practical advantages. Because idleness has been eliminated in Utopia, with everyone being devoted to productive tasks, there are more workers available, which in turn makes possible a reduction in the length of the working day. Also, the simplicity of the Utopian way of life requires less total labor than in other countries. The Utopians thus enjoy more leisure for the pursuit of innocent pleasures and the culture of the mind (133/12–135/23).

Such a rationally ordered social system could run the risk of appearing austere and remote (and many students commonly feel that it does), but More tries to avoid this by giving it a human face. His description of the Utopians' common meals, in particular, gives fleeting glimpses of individuals amongst them: the syphogrant and his wife sitting at the middle of the high table; the men with their backs to the wall at a table down the side of the hall, so arranged as to allow a woman who is pregnant to get up without disturbing others if she has a sudden qualm or pain; the nurses and infants in a separate dining room, playing in front of a warm fire; older boys and girls waiting on the tables, at which older people are seated in conspicuous places so that they can be served first (141/36 – 145/5). These and other details humanize the image we have of Utopian society and project Utopia as being a very happy place. The total impression is further enhanced by references to the innocent pleasures that grace Utopian meals: the music that accompanies the evening meal, the delicacies that form the dessert, and the Utopians' practice of burning incense and scattering perfume (145/20–26). By incorporating all these humane details into the description of his philosophical city, More is clearly trying to ensure (at this stage in book 2) that it leaves a favorable impression in the minds of his readers—as, indeed, for the most part, it has.

HINTS OF AMBIVALENCE

Yet for all More's efforts to make his eutopia as attractive as possible, he could not avoid the consequences of possessing the kind of consciousness that recognizes both the positive and negative sides of any issue at once. From the moment he began to create a

ity of his language suggests, paradoxically, that the very features that make Utopia seem desirable may, in fact, furnish a reason to mistrust it. Although it seems ideally secure, it may be so protected from the vicissitudes of real life that it is ultimately ineffectual as a model. In short, the rational perfection by which it is ordered may promote nothing more than social stagnation.

This is the latent doubt in More's own mind concerning his creation. It surfaces time and again in countless instances of linguistic ambiguity that no English translation can ever hope to reproduce. Even the apparently innocent name he invented for the officials who rule over every group of 30 households contains a seed for its own ironic subversion. The Greek-derived *phylarchus* can mean "head of a tribe," but it can also mean "fond of rule or power" (389, note to 114/7). Although it is true, as the Yale editor points out, that the ambitious man has no place in Utopian government, the ironic double meaning in More's coined word neatly captures his latent fear that it might prove impossible, even in the best society, to restrain the human appetite for the power that comes with such positions. Given that More had an intense loathing of tyranny all through his life, it is not surprising that he may have harbored a secret doubt that he was supplying the officials in his visionary society with the means of exercising it.

More's latent capacity for experiencing doubt also surfaces in his use of the rhetorical figure of litotes—the device of affirming something by stating the negative of its opposite.[2] Thus the Utopians have clothes that are "not unbecoming to the eye" (*nec ad oculum indecora*) (126/5) and live in houses that are "in no way mean" (*neutiquam sordida*) (120/4). They elect their tranibors annually but change them "not . . . without good reason" (*Caeterum haud temere commutant*) (122/21). Agriculture is the one occupation "which no one does not share in" (*cuius nemo est expers*) (124/21–22). The usefulness of litotes is that it does not require one to formulate the positive of what is actually being affirmed. Consequently, it is a figure of thought that lends itself ideally for the expression of ambiguity. We can see this in all the instances quoted above. To say that Utopian clothes are "not unbecoming to the eye" allows for a doubt that they may, in fact, be a bit drab, even if they are not downright unbecoming. So too with the houses;

to say that they are "in no way mean" is to stop short of positively affirming that they are the most splendid that could be built.

The other two examples of litotes are slightly more disturbing in the suggestions they set free. To assert that agriculture is the one pursuit "that no one does not share in" implies that this shared pursuit might not be as voluntary in all cases, were a degree of compulsion not present. Lurking behind the rhetorical figure may be More's suspicion that human nature will not naturally lend itself to the support of the system he has devised, unless it is forced to do so. The same is true of the statement that the Utopians change their tranibors "not without good reason." Without explicitly saying what those good reasons might be, More allows for the chance that there might be some, and in a paragraph that has just mentioned governors who are ousted "on suspicion of aiming at a tyranny" (123/20–21), it is not too hard to guess what they are: the litotes betrays More's fear, here as elsewhere, that human nature will find ways of evading the constraints of his system so as to abuse it.

The detection of what I have called More's "ambifocalism" might be dismissed as the fantasy of a critic who had been exposed for too long to the propaganda of modern deconstructive theory, were it not for the fact that this dual focus appears explicitly in the shadowy ironic parallel More develops between England and Utopia. As the marginal glosses underline, "London agrees with Amaurotum" in many details, not least in the broad tidal river that flows through it, the magnificently arched stone bridge that links one side of the city to the other, and its high, broad wall with towers and battlements (119/1–39). Just as pertinently, the island itself resembles England in being separated from the adjoining continent by a channel. Utopia, like England, has also been subjugated by a conqueror who has instituted the system of administration on which the society is founded. As our gaze penetrates through the superficial appearance of Utopia, then, we see England residing within it, as if the image of one has been superimposed on the other in a way that makes it difficult to disentangle the aspects that might belong to the one or the other.

The import of this dual-focused image is highly ambiguous. Does it serve to remind us of England for the sake of strengthening our awareness of the radical contrast between (evil) Europe and (enlightened) Utopia that the work is ostensibly developing? Or is it

designed to suggest that, at a deeper level, there are hidden similarities in the experience of Utopia and England—similarities that
are ultimately more significant than the more visible differences?
We are never told the answer to this question, and its resolution is
made all the more impossible by the fact that each of the two narrators, Hythlodaeus and "More," eventually reaches different
conclusions concerning it.

The one thing we can be sure of is that, by the time More had
completed his exposition of the social system of Utopia, he was
thoroughly aware that his vision of an ideal state had the capacity
to dissolve and reconstitute itself as an image of its direct opposite.
He came to see that there was potentially a negative aspect to
almost every "ideal" arrangement he could contrive for his commonwealth, and as he came to see this he had to control an urge to
ironize the product of his own idealistic imagination.

While it is in the middle section of book 2 that More surrendered most fully to this urge, there are several early signs in the
first section of the reaction to come. The most striking example of it
is the short passage describing the Utopians' method of raising
poultry: "They breed a vast quantity of poultry by a wonderful con-
trivance. The hens do not brood over the eggs, but the farmers, by
keeping a great number of them at a uniform heat, bring them to
life and hatch them. As soon as they come out of the shell, the
chicks follow and acknowledge humans as their mothers!"
(115/25–31). It is likely that More took his cue for this anecdote
from Bernard von Breydenbach's account of Egyptian incubators in
his widely popular *Peregrinatio in Terram Sanctam*.[3] Whatever his
source, More placed his anecdote at this point in the narrative in
order to create the image of a practice that intercepts the natural
course of things so as to modify it through artifice. Given that he
has just finished describing Utopia's rational distribution of cities
and households, the description of the artificial incubation of eggs
serves as a symbolic comment on what has gone before. In effect,
the passage is pinpointing, with a degree of comic irony, the essential features of Utopia that make More's "ideal" society possible: its
artificial engineering of nature, and especially human nature, and
the rather drab uniformity and conformity that necessarily follow.

This chicken-hatching anecdote also furnishes an analogy with
the Utopians' method of artificially regulating their population by

transferring individuals from one household and city to another, and by transplanting superfluous individuals to colonies on the mainland (135/35–137/22). These practices have good classical precedent (they can be found in Plato's *Laws* [5.740A–41A]), but however rational and efficient they may be, More can hardly have been unaware of the antipathy that the whole idea of such regulation would arouse in those of his readers who valued their own human relationships. It is almost as if More presented these ideas as provocation, to show in humane terms the real consequences of applying ideally rational principles.

In short, More discovered that his *eutopia* ("happy place") was indeed a *utopia* ("no place"), for it could never be solely happy without potentially also being unhappy—human nature saw to that. As Erasmus wrote in *The Praise of Folly*, "All human affairs are like the figures of Silenus. . . . [Y]ou'll find everything suddenly reversed if you open the Silenus" (*Erasmus*, 27: 102–3). By the end of the first section of book 2 of *Utopia*, More had opened the Silenus of his creation and saw how it had the potential to turn inside out. The effect of this on More's attitude toward his creation is reflected in one small textual variant that can easily escape notice. At the climax of the first section, just after Hythlodaeus has delivered his first enthusiastic eulogy of Utopia, the 1516 edition refers to Amaurotum as "Mentirano"—the "City of Lies."[4] It would seem that at some stage More had either thought of calling the capital of Utopia Mentirano or else had already given it that name and subsequently changed his mind, the textual variant being a slip that had escaped his attention during revision. Be that as it may, the irony contained within the variant name is unequivocal and suggestive: what one is seeing in Utopia may be a lie—the product of false appearances. For the sake of expounding the social ideals nearest to his heart, he kept any ambivalence he may have felt concerning his equivocal commonwealth largely suppressed during this first section, but the lid came off, as it was bound to do, when he decided to pass on to an account of Utopian ethics. It was at this point that he surrendered to the satiric sense of irony and paradox that had been brewing in him ever since he gave his imagination free play.

6

Incursions of Doubt:
Irony and Satire in Book 2

Even though More's vision of Utopia was equivocal from the beginning, while he was expounding the sociopolitical base of his ideally
rational state he was able to keep any doubts he may have felt
about it largely suppressed. Even the opening eutopian section of
book 2, however, contains ironies, as we have seen, that betray
More's awareness of things capable of subverting the viability of his
model: (a) the paradox that what may seem desirable to human
reason may equally seem detestable at the level of humane feeling
and emotion, and (b) an inherent bias in human nature toward evil
that will become progressively more apparent as book 2 proceeds.
These awarenesses are not heavily insisted on in the early part of
book 2, but they are present nevertheless.

More could have ended *Utopia* there: with the exposition of an
imaginary socioeconomic eutopia that would excite his humanist
contemporaries but that nevertheless contained a sufficient number of implicit ironies to protect him against any charge of political
naïveté. He chose to continue, however, not only to deal with
Utopian ethics and religion but (in book 1) to reactivate the peren-
nial dispute over whether a wise man should participate in politics
or not. We must ask ourselves why.

One reason is that More would have known from his reading of
Plato and Aristotle that the political philosopher needed to determine what constitutes the happiest life for the individual.[1] In his
prescription for constructing an ideal commonwealth, Aristotle

declared, "We ought . . . to ascertain, first of all, which is the most generally eligible life."[2] More had done that: he had determined that the most generally eligible life was one lived in common. Aristotle also, however, had stated that the happy man should enjoy not only external goods and goods of the body but also the goods of the soul. Furthermore, he had raised difficult questions about the sources of happiness, and the relative superiority of this or that good. To compound matters, he had also questioned "whether the happiness of the individual is the same as that of the state, or different," and whether "the life of business and politics is or is not more desirable than one which is wholly independent of external goods, [i.e.,] a contemplative life, which by some is maintained to be the only one worthy of a philosopher" (*Politics*, 158). Given More's competitive instincts and his natural hubris—the urge to "prove masteries" that would be displayed so terrifyingly when he came to write his religious polemics—a desire to emulate his predecessors, if not outdo them, may have impelled him to go on.

A further reason may be that More had already seen too deeply into his visionary society to lie about it. The very act of devising a local habitation and name for his ideal state had shown him that the definitive rational reform of society is ultimately impossible. One person's ideal is another's nightmare, and different people are always likely to disagree as to which is which in any case. He could not, therefore, allow it to appear as if he regarded Utopian polity as an ideal model when he knew it was not. More was reluctant, however, to relinquish totally the blueprint for a society toward which he had felt so deeply drawn. To the extent that he was attracted to his own invention, he seems to have felt it necessary to disguise the appeal it had for him. Whatever the reason, More ventured beyond his account of Utopian economics and politics to expound Utopian ethics.

The result finally sealed the fate of his imaginary exemplum. As More let his imagination construct the kind of ethical system a society might devise on the basis of sheer reason, he became aware of a massive contradiction between the findings of reason and certain religious beliefs and practices of Christianity that had evolved through the medieval centuries. His response was to distance himself still further from his imaginative creation by introducing yet more irony. This was designed to act partly as a corrective to any excesses in his enthusiasm and partly as a screen capable of protecting him from the gaze of those who might perceive the extent to which he had been drawn to a mode of social living of which he could not allow himself intellectually to approve. From this point on, Utopia changed rapidly from a eutopia to a place with absurd and even dystopian elements in its very fabric, until by the end of the second section of book 2 the exemplum had turned itself inside out to become a utopia—a "nowhere" that is paradoxically "everywhere" and a reformed society that shows why society cannot ultimately be reformed, even while affirming that the attempt to reform it must nevertheless be made.

SHIFTING PARADOXES

When More launched into his description of Utopian moral principles and ethical practices, he seems at first to have believed that he could use the Utopians to develop a simple paradox. According to Renaissance literary theory, one type of paradox could be created by developing an argument contrary to received opinion. In this middle section of *Utopia* More does that with a vengeance. By setting up the Utopians as a foil to Europeans, he is able to castigate Europeans because of the moral criticism implied by the contrast. The Utopians, for example, have a healthy contempt for precious metals. Whereas Europeans constantly strive to accumulate gold and silver, the Utopians, we are told, consider these metals to be inferior to iron and make their chamber pots and humblest vessels out of them. Gold and silver are also used to make the chains and shackles of slaves and bear the stigma of disgrace (153/4–20). The glossator fully appreciates the wit of these playful inversions and draws our attention to it in several marginal comments: "O Artful Rogue!" (151/7), "O Magnificent Affront to Gold!" (153/6). In such cases More is clearly using the Utopians as a stick with which to beat Europeans for their presumed cupidity and materialism.

This device achieves its fullest potential in the story of the Anemolian ("Windy") ambassadors who visited Utopia. Not realizing the contempt shown by the Utopians toward gold, silver, and precious stones, the three Anemolian emissaries made a grand entry arrayed in cloth of gold, festooned with gold chains, jewels in their ears, and strings of pearls and gems on their caps. More propounds this episode as a grand joke at the expense of the Anemolians who, like Europeans, base their credibility on the material substance they are able to display. The fall line is almost too predictable: Utopian children poke and nudge their mothers and comment on the childishness of these adults who still believe that material ostentation has any effect when, as adults, they should have grown out of any such self-deceptions (155/3 – 157/11).

But More must have wondered whom he was trying to fool, for even while he was trying to invest the Utopians with ethical values that would rebuke Europeans for their moral turpitude, his growing mistrust of his own idealistic model surfaced once again with renewed vigor. We see it in the appearance of a new, much more complicated type of paradox than the commonplace kind I have just described.

The new kind of paradox might best be described as "situational paradox"—a kind of paradox generated by the presentation of incongruities arising from the application of moral principles that should preclude them.[3] In this middle section of book 2, such paradox appears, for example, in the fact that the Utopians' contempt for material wealth leaves them with more of it than even the most acquisitive of European societies. Furthermore, the way in which they spend it demonstrates the presence of the very same self-interest that they are trying to avoid. Being able to accumulate an immense treasury, they promptly spend it on the hiring of foreign mercenaries, at extravagant rates of pay, for they would far sooner risk mercenaries in battle against their enemies than their own citizens. Moreover, they shrewdly perceive that the enemy's soldiers can either be bought off or else set at odds with one another through payments of money (149/33 – 151/3). Whether they know it or not, the Utopians are playing upon the intrinsic evil in human nature for their own advantage. Theoretically, if they were truly motivated by the humane compassion and charity they profess, they should be just as concerned to control these sinful impulses in the citizens of their neighboring countries as in their own. Their unwillingness to do so shows that they are prepared to live cynically according to a double standard. By including such a detail about Utopia More is implicitly confessing that the competitive and self-assertive instincts of human nature are ultimately more powerful than the moral codes by which any idealistic humanist theorist might try to restrain them.

Once More had allowed such paradoxes to surface in his Utopian exemplum there was very little point in trying to sustain the society's credibility as an ideal. Recognizing this, More gave up any pretense at maintaining a stable, consistent norm in *Utopia* and was content instead to range freely through every degree of approbation and disapprobation, for the most part taking care to disguise from the reader which is which.

More's description of Utopian moral philosophy is a case in point. In it we can see a pattern of shifting intellectual perspectives on the part of the author that will recur throughout this middle section and that betrays the extent to which his idealistic vision was susceptible to destabilization. The Utopians at first seem to have made an admirable fist of reconciling the basic conflicts found in European moral philosophy. Although they carry on the same argument as to whether the name "good" can be applied to the goods of the body and external gifts (the Aristotelian position) as well as the goods of the mind (the Stoic view) (161/17–22), they seem to have reconciled the deep conflict between the Aristotelian and Stoic positions. The Aristotelian view promotes a much greater concern with the material requirements of the body than does the Stoic view, which, in its greater emphasis on the mind's self-contained integrity, readily promotes an attitude of *contemptus mundi* (contempt of the world).

By inclining toward a modified version of Epicureanism the Utopians try to avoid the potential conflict between the two attitudes. True happiness, they aver, consists of pleasure; moreover, they reinforce the philosophical rationalism that leads them to this proposition with certain principles drawn from their religion: namely, that (a) the soul of man is immortal and (b) that after this life virtue is rewarded and vice punished (161/25–163/5). By invoking these religious beliefs, they extend the bounds of classical Epicureanism to encompass the life of the soul as well as that of the body (Epicurus had assumed that the soul was mortal), and by adding to them a further notion that there is a hierarchy of greater and lesser pleasures, the Utopians make their Epicureanism compatible not only with the Stoic belief that happiness resides in virtue but also with the Christian view that an otherworldly heaven is where true happiness lies. Thus they justify their pursuit of the good society in this world without discarding the spiritual idealism of those philosophies that see the ultimate goal of human endeavor as being in the next world.

Such eclecticism might strike many readers as too good to be true, and More seems to have believed so too, for signs of his habitual equivocation soon begin to appear. They surface first in an insistent syntactical repetition that draws readers' attention to a possible flaw in the Utopian argument. In opening his discussion of Utopian philosophy, More had described their chief debate as concerning the nature of true "happiness" (*felicitas*) (161/23–25). Very quickly, however, he makes us aware that they are in danger of confusing their terms. The word *happiness* is soon replaced with "joy" (*iucunditas*), and that, in turn, is repeatedly equated with the concept of "pleasure" (*voluptas*). We might not even notice this if the syntax did not so insistently draw attention to it through the repetitions it presents:

> . . . if it is especially humane . . . to relieve the misery of others and, by taking away all sadness from their life, restore them *to enjoyment, that is, to pleasure.* (163/36–39) (. . . *uittae* iucunditati, *hoc est* uoluptati *reddere.*) [my emphasis]

> . . . either *a joyous life, that is, a pleasurable life,* is evil. (165/3) (. . . *aut mala est uitta* iucunda, *id est,* uoluptaria.) [my emphasis]

> So nature herself, they maintain, prescribes to us *a joyous life or, in other words, pleasure,* as the end of all our operations. (165/13–14) (*Vitam ergo* iucundam *inquiunt, id est* uoluptatem *tanquam operationum omnium finem.*) [my emphasis]

These repeated syntactical equations make us aware that an important question is being begged: Is "joy," in fact, ultimately to be equated with "pleasure," let alone "happiness"? Furthermore, how do any of these things relate to *gaudium* ("spiritual gladness"), a concept that the Utopians at one point (166/3) invoke?

The ensuing discussion of true and false pleasures seems to hold out the possibility that the Utopians have got it right—in terms

of ordinary human desires and, possibly, More's own wistful inclinations. Although the Utopians reject (as the glossator highlights)
mistaken pride in ostentatious clothing, foolish honors, gems,
dicing, and hunting (167–73), they extol as *true* pleasures good
health, strength, beauty, and agility on the physical side and sat-
isfaction from the practice of virtue and the consciousness of a
good life on the intellectual side (173–75). All this strikes the reader
as very attractive in its humane, life-accepting rationality.

As one has been led to expect, nevertheless, More's habitual
equivocation begins to surface with renewed force. Having
attributed to the Utopians a "joyous acceptance" of bodily
pleasures—provided that a lesser pleasure does not get in the way
of a greater one and that no "pleasure" produces pain in its aftermath (177/27–37)—More immediately (and paradoxically) allows for
circumstances in which pain and privation may indeed produce
pleasure. While he affirms that the Utopians think it a sign of
"extreme madness and the sign of a mind which is both cruel to
itself and ungrateful to nature" to "despise the beauty of form, to
impair the strength of the body, to turn nimbleness into sluggish-
ness, to exhaust the body by fasts, to injure one's health, and to
reject all the other favors of nature," he nevertheless concedes that,
by so doing, a man or a woman may sometimes serve the good of
other persons or of the public (177/38– 179/4).

The conditional word *otherwise* (*alioquin*) (178/4) signals a
renewed onset of the skepticism that subverts any positive proposal
that More makes in *Utopia* as soon as he has come to the point of
formulating it explicitly. Having just introduced a qualification that
potentially undermines the whole philosophy he has just
expounded with such care, he immediately follows it up with an
escape clause allowing him to remove himself from what he has
just imaginatively proposed. As a kind of peroration for the section
on Utopian ethics, he has Hythlodaeus conclude, "This is their view
of virtue and pleasure." They believe that "human reason can attain
to no truer view, unless a heaven-sen treligion inspire man with
something more holy. Whether in this stand they are right or
wrong, time does not permit us to examine—nor is it necessary. We
have taken upon ourselves only to describe their principles, and
not also to defend them" (179/12–18). By stating this, More
successfully distances himself from any complicity in the

philosophy his narrative persona has just described—as something safely observed in the antipodes. Nevertheless, More's disappointment in the collapse of his private vision is manifest in other significant ways.

ATTEMPTS AT AUTHORIAL DISTANCING

As was the case in the first section of book 2 of *Utopia*, More finds ways in the second section to distance himself from any aspects of Utopia, even those he had appeared to expound enthusiastically, of which his consciousness would not ultimately let him approve. In particular, he goes to some length to distance himself from Utopian ethics once he has admitted the qualifications that threaten to sub-vert the Utopians' effort to resolve the contradictions of Western philosophy.

As usual, More's first self-extracting ploy is to retreat into Lucianic facetiousness, the onset of which he heralds by introduc-ing the merry tale of the monkey who ripped up a work by Theophrastus that Hythlodaeus had taken to the Utopians (181/36). More quickly follows this up by introducing another of the punning ironic names he had used in the first section ("Mentirano," "Amaurotum," "phylarchus," etc.). This time the pun occurs in the name assigned to one of Hythlodaeus's companions on the voyage, "Tricius Apinatus" (183/6). The name is drawn from a statement by Martial, the Roman satirical poet, to the effect that Martial's epigrams are *"apinae tricaeque"* (trifles and toys) (*Utopia*, ed. Logan and Adams, 78, note 76). This allusion invites the learned reader thereafter to take the philosophical disquisition with minimal seriousness.

To extract himself still further, More uses another of his typical devices—to furnish several instances of reductio ad absurdum of the propositions he had been propounding. The first instance occurs immediately after the description of the Utopian system of slavery (signalled in the text by a separate heading). The fact that the section on slavery does not seem to spring naturally from the discussion on ethics might suggest that at this point a seam had been opened in More's first draft. Be that as it may, when More abruptly passes to describe the Utopians' treatment of their sick people, he picks up on the pleasure principle that animates Utopian philosophy and shows how the way that the Utopians apply it raises questions as to whether it is valid at all.

Because they believe happiness resides in pleasure, they are reluctant to let their citizens experience pain. This is manifest in their treatment of the incurably ill. While everything possible is done to ease sick a person's pain, if the disease is incurable and "agonizing without any cessation" (187/5) the priests exhort that person to commit suicide (auto-euthanasia), since he or she is "unequal to all life's duties, a burden to himself [or herself], and a trouble to others" (187/7–10). This is, of course, the logical outcome of a philosophy predicated on a belief in pleasure as the source of happiness, but it does not sit easily with the idea of More as a father who, as William Roper tells us, was so distressed at his mistaken assumption that his daughter Margaret would die from sleeping sickness that he swore that, should she die, "he would never have meddled with worldly matters after" (Roper, 28–29). Logic may dictate that people should kill themselves if they are suffering so much that they believe they may not recover, but More must have known he was playing on strong, complex emotions.

The second reductio ad absurdum occurs in the description of the practice whereby the Utopians exhibit prospective marriage partners to one another, naked:

> They . . . marvelled at the remarkable folly of all other nations. In buying a colt, where there is question of only a little money, persons are so cautious that though it is almost bare they will not buy until they have taken off the saddle and removed all the trappings for fear some sore lies concealed under these coverings. Yet in the choice of a wife, an action which will cause either pleasure or disgust to follow them the rest of their lives, they are so careless that, while the rest of her body is covered with clothes, they estimate the value of the whole woman from hardly a single handbreadth of her, only the face being visible, and clasp her to themselves not without great danger of their agreeing ill together if something afterwards gives them offense. (189/6–17)

Even though this sentiment is closely modeled on a passage in St. Jerome's *Epistola adversus Jovinianum* (either directly or indirectly

through Chaucer),[4] it seems placed in the narrative to provoke out-
rage, while nevertheless assuming the appearance of a mere joke.
As if to give a cue to readers, More has Hythlodaeus observe that
this custom "seemed to us very foolish and extremely ridiculous"
(189/1). The fact that More included it at all betrays his awareness
that the moral philosophy he had given the Utopians might not
stand the scrutiny of those who believed in human dignity.

The pattern evident in the whole of book 2's middle section is
seen in microcosm in local descriptions, particularly of the Utopian
attitude toward marriage and divorce. The Utopians, we are told,
consider marriage to be inviolable under *ordinary circumstances*.
On grounds of adultery or "intolerable offensiveness of disposition"
(189/27–31), however, they are forced to allow separation. Within a
few sentences, we are told that the fundamental principle is allowed
to break down still further: "When a married couple agree insuffi-
ciently in their dispositions and both find others with whom they
hope to live more agreeably, *they separate by mutual consent* and
contract fresh unions" (191/1–4; my italics). The absolute ideal rule
that More had initially proposed is, therefore, shown to break down
rapidly under the pressure of human experience.

What, in fact, we are seeing in the second section of book 2 is
the exact same tendency in the process of More's imaginative literary creation that had manifested itself in the opening section: he
first professes a hypothetical ideal, then undermines the ideal
through ironic facetiousness, and finally subverts the ideal altogether by subjecting it to a reductio ad absurdum that either presents the ideal as a pious illusion or else provokes the reader to
question it on more subtle emotive grounds. The second section
differs from the first, however, in that the skepticism More
acknowledges strikes a lot deeper—into the very heart of the
"utopian" endeavor.

THE DESCENT INTO SATIRIC IRONY

This more serious level of subversion is revealed in a gradual
transformation of More's facetious, Lucianic irony into a more bitter
and severe form of satiric irony. We see it especially in the passages

describing the measures the Utopians adopt when they go to war. As usual, the ideal principle is announced first: "War, as an activity fit only for beasts . . . they regard with utter loathing" (199/36–37). Within a couple sentences, however, subversion of this principle sets in with the information that, out of "human sympathy," the Utopians go to war for several just causes: to protect their own territory, to drive an invading enemy from their friends' lands, or to deliver oppressed people from the yoke of tyranny (201/5–9). Soon we are told that they also go to war sometimes "to requite and avenge injuries previously done to them" (201/11–12). Thus despite professing an ideal attitude toward war, the Utopians quickly find that experience seduces them into acting out of the worst of motives. Ultimately, they find that they are trapped within the limitations of human nature, just like everyone else. Even when they believe that they are acting altruistically, their interventions produce tragic results:

> Such was the origin of the war which the Utopians had waged a little before our time on behalf of the Nephelogetes against the Alaopolitans. The Nephelogetic traders suffered a wrong, as they thought, under pretence of law, but whether right or wrong, it was avenged by a fierce war. Into this war the neighboring nations brought their energies and resources to assist the power and to intensify the rancor of both sides. Most flourishing nations were either shaken to their foundations or grievously afflicted. The troubles upon troubles that arose were ended only by the enslavement and surrender of the Alaopolitans. Since the Utopians were not fighting in their own interest, they yielded them into the power of the Nephelogetes, a people who, when the Alaopolitans were prosperous, were not in the least comparable to them. (201/21–33)

Here again is another reductio ad absurdum that shows how easily attempts to act according to an ideal principle can produce consequences opposite to those intended. The Utopians discover that they are no less subject to the imperfections of human nature, and of the human situation, than the rest of humanity.

This seems to have been the realization that resurfaced and proved fatal to More's own utopianism while he was writing book 2. No matter which aspect of human experience he treated, he sooner or later came up against the fact that human nature is irremediably imperfect and therefore produces human responses to experience that are bound to be likewise imperfect, whether this imperfection manifests itself in a stubborn refusal to be strictly rational or in the execution of deeds that are distinctly evil.

In the section on Utopian warfare More brings the full implications of this realization to the fore by allowing Utopian war practices to display the evil in human nature at its most terrifying. As soon as war is declared, the Utopians offer huge bribes for the assassination of the enemy king; if this does not work, they sow seeds of dissension by fostering rival claimants to the throne or by reviving forgotten disputes between the enemy country and its neighbors; they hire mercenaries, but if they have to fight themselves they surround each man on the battlefield with his own children and relations by marriage, so that he will fight with all the more incentive and ferocity; if the enemy stands his ground, "the battle is long and anguished and ends with mutual extermination" (203/36–211/10). It is almost as if, by showing these things, More aimed to shock any readers inclined to idealize the Utopians. Ironically, each of the war strategies they adopt were actually practiced by European nations in More's time, and altogether they seem remarkably similar to the evil advice Hythlodaeus describes as being given to the French king, in book 1 (87/26–89/22).

The closeness of the parallel between European and Utopian war practices heightens the essential irony that More has been developing throughout this central section of book 2—that despite superficial differences Europe and Utopia share at least as much in common as they diverge from each other. In fact, the exemplum has been gradually turning itself inside out, until a point is reached at which the initial relationship between Europe and Utopia, which was one of antithesis, is entirely inverted. This occurs when Hythlodaeus recounts the Utopians' refusal to enter into treaties:

> They are led to this opinion chiefly because in those parts of the world treaties and alliances between kings are not observed with much good faith. In Europe, however, and especially in those parts where the faith and religion of Christ prevails, the majesty of treaties is everywhere holy and inviolable, partly through the justice and goodness of kings, partly through the reverence and fear of the Sovereign Pontiffs. . . . But in that new world, which is

almost as far removed from ours by the equator as their life and
character are different from ours, there is no trust in treaties.
(197/24–39)

Whereas More had initially set Europe in contrast with Utopia to
the discredit of the former, here he is pretending to set Europe in
contrast with Utopia to the discredit of the latter, while nevertheless meaning the exact opposite of what he says. The result is a
very crude and bitter sort of satiric irony that has not yet been seen
in the work, and its very presence suggests that More was lashing
out at the failure of his "ideal" model to deliver all he had fancifully
expected from it. Put another way, instead of being the instruments
of satire, the Utopians had now become the object of satire. It is not
insignificant that by this point in book 2 the glossator, who had
been so enthusiastic in his marginal glosses to the earlier part of
the work, has practically fallen silent, which may imply the unease
that More's desperate authorial reaction may have produced in
him. As far as the bellicose side of Utopian life is concerned, there
is little for most people to be enthusiastic about.

The plain truth of the matter is that by the time he finished the
middle section of book 2, More had found his political and social
idealism subverted by his abiding sense of the sinfulness of human
nature and the imperfectibility of the human situation at large. He
had become aware that the Utopian "eutopia" he was propounding
could only exist among peoples removed from all contact with the
conditions that ordinary human societies must confront—an
awareness implicit in his whimsical notion that King Utopus had
caused Utopia to be separated from its mainland via a man-made
channel (113/8–18). But by the time More came to deal with
Utopian warfare, he was prepared to concede that in any human
culture a nation such as Utopia would be likely to encounter foreign neighbors who would bring the Utopians forcefully into contact
with the sinfulness of human nature, however successfully they
might seem to have suppressed sinful impulses within the boundaries of their own society.

On completing the middle section of book 2 of *Utopia*, More
faced a major problem. Once he had admitted human imperfection
into his eutopia he found that his visionary commonwealth had

turned into Utopia—"nowhere" indeed. He was not prepared to concede, however, that his visionary idealism had no purpose or that the larger paradox captured in the title of his work attested merely to a cosmic joke at the expense of humankind. Instead, he was concerned to find a way in which the Utopians' experience of frustration, and his own, could be viewed as creative and purposeful in a larger providential scheme. That is precisely what he did in resolving the Utopians' dilemma at the level of their religious experience.

7

Confidence Restored:
Religious Faith in Utopia

As demonstrated in the previous chapter, by the time More had
finished writing the middle section of book 2 of *Utopia* his exemplum had practically turned itself inside out. The earlier part of
Hythlodaeus's narrative had hinted at similarities between Utopia
and Europe (such as the geographical parallels between England
and Utopia and Amaurotum and London) so as to offset the more
significant differences: especially, the extreme contrast between
Utopian and European social practices. This rhetorical strategy had
progressively altered its complexion, so that by the time More had
come to describe the Utopian attitude toward treaties and warfare
the opposite was true: *similarities* between Utopian and European
practices are placed in the foreground, so that any differences serve
merely to highlight the more significant parallels. More's rhetorical
procedure had thus reversed itself.

Indeed, when Hythlodaeus is describing the Utopians' attitude
toward treaties we see a kind of inverted double irony that shows
just how radically More had replaced the earlier set of interpretative
cues he had been offering to readers with another set diametrically
opposed to the first. The Utopians, we are told, make no treaties
with other nations, because "in those parts of the world treaties
and alliances between kings are not observed with much good
faith." In Europe, on the other hand, especially where the Christian
faith and religion prevail, "the majesty of treaties is everywhere holy
and inviolable, partly through the justice and goodness of kings,

partly through the reverence and fear of the Sovereign Pontiffs" (197/26–30). More thus appears to be drawing a contrast between Utopia and Europe in the way to which the reader has become accustomed, but this time to the advantage of the latter. He even goes as far as to draw attention to this ostensible contrast he is pretending to make: "in that new world, which is almost as far removed from ours by the equator as their life and character are different from ours, there is no trust in treaties" (197/37–39).

While appearing to draw an explicit contrast, he is nevertheless saying the very opposite of what he means in order to establish an implicit *equation* between the two societies. Put another way, More is attributing to Europeans the virtuous attitude that, according to the initial rhetorical strategy of the paradigm, one would have expected the Utopians to have, in order to consolidate readers' awareness that neither the Europeans nor the Utopians have such an attitude. More's willingness to do such a thing by this point in book 2 is illuminating, for it shows the extent to which he had lost faith in his visionary society's ability to sustain the burden of idealistic expectation he had originally placed on it. Such a change of heart in More helps explain why generations of readers have felt uncertain as to how they are being invited to respond to *Utopia*.

Had More left his narrative at this point, book 2 would have simply confirmed that the skepticism inherent in his utopianism was ultimately more powerful than the idealism it accompanied, and that the utopian vision itself was a failure. Should this have occurred, More would merely have been reverting to the pessimistic worldview he had earlier been tempted to adopt. In several juvenile poems written a decade earlier, he had concluded that the world was wholly under the influence of Fortune, and that Fortune was not merely inconstant but deliberately malicious: "she kepeth euer in store, / From euery manne some parcell of his wyll, / That he may pray therfore and serue her styll."[1] The failure of his imaginary state to escape from limitations imposed on it by the world's imperfection was, one suspects, tempting More to retreat into his former pessimism—a temptation manifest most clearly in the radical transformations of perspective and tone that lead to the bitter satiric irony of the passages describing Utopian war practices. More did not succumb to this impulse, however, and this chapter attempts to explain why.

PROVIDENTIAL SIGNS

Having shown the failure of the Utopians to translate their ideal principles into perfect social and moral results, More was faced with a choice: he could either allow his exemplum to crumble under the weight of its own negative implications, or else he could seek some way of accounting for the imperfections he had uncovered in it, in terms that would allow Utopian experience to be viewed as positive rather than negative, and as giving greater cause for hope than despair. He chose to do the latter, by propounding for the Utopians a set of religious beliefs and practices that allow even the limitations and imperfections of their endeavors to be seen as purposeful within a divine providential scheme.

Utopian religion depends on two fundamental beliefs: that the soul is immortal and will be rewarded for virtue or punished for vice after death, and that the universe is governed by divine providence (221/30–34). The first belief gives Utopians an incentive to strive after goodness, while the second enables them to acknowledge a beneficent purpose in the experience they undergo, including the frustration of their idealistic utopianism. In particular, they are able to see the hand of providence in their history—not only their religious history but also their secular history. Their annals record how they have become transformed from a rude and rustic rabble into almost the most humane and cultured people in the world (113/5–8). They have achieved this not only by exercising goodwill but also by seizing on the opportunities presented by emergent occasions. In A.D. 315, for instance, some Romans and Egyptians were shipwrecked on the Utopian coast, an event that the inhabitants were quick to exploit: "Now mark what good advantage their industry took of this one opportunity. The Roman empire possessed no art capable of any use which they did not either learn from the shipwrecked strangers or discover for themselves after receiving the hints for investigation" (109/6–10). Similarly, when Hythlodaeus and his European companions arrive in Utopia, the inhabitants eagerly absorb the classical authors brought to them by the travelers and learn how to make paper and print letters, whereas previously they had only been able to write on parchment, bark, and papyrus: "Their first attempts were not very successful, but by frequent experiment they soon mastered both" (183/36–37).

This detail shows what is positive in the Utopians' response to history. They are able to see life as an ongoing process that invites behavior that is relatively convenient for a particular time, rather than definitively determined for all time. Above all, they recognize that new possibilities are continuously likely to emerge as providence, according to divine wisdom, decides to present them.

This attitude is manifest even more clearly in the Utopians' religious history. There are, we learn, many different forms of religion throughout Utopia: some inhabitants worship the sun as a god, or the moon, or other planets, while others worship a man who was conspicuous for either virtue or glory in the past. The vast majority, however, believe in "a certain single being, unknown, eternal, immense, inexplicable, far above the reach of the human mind, diffused throughout the universe not in mass but in power" (217/6–15). Quite deliberately, More seems to have attributed to the Utopians many aspects of the religious phenomena recorded in the history of the known world. Those among the Utopians who worship the sun, moon, or other planets are like the Egyptians or Persians, while those who worship distinguished men of virtue or glory are like pre-Christian Romans. The Utopians are similar, too, to medieval Europeans in the way that gradually "they are all beginning to depart from this medley of superstitions and are coming to unite in that one religion which seems to surpass the rest in reasonableness" (217/2–29). More even suggests an implicit parallel between the Utopians and Europeans by showing that in each hemisphere the shedding of superstition is retarded by fear of supernatural retribution. Just as many Romans, according to St. Augustine, interpreted the fall of the eternal city to the barbarians as a punishment on men for abandoning the old gods,[2] so too do some Utopians, Hythlodaeus tells us, interpret various misfortunes as having been visited on them by the offended deity whom they have been intending to forsake (217/29–35).

Thus, the pattern that More highlights in Utopia's religious experience is, like that revealed in its people's secular history, one that involves a dynamic and evolutionary process. It reveals a movement away from pagan superstition and toward a less primitive form of conduct that can best be described as proto-Christian. Indeed, one of the reasons that the Utopians prove so extremely receptive to Christianity is that it is "nearest to that belief which has the widest prevalence among them" (219/4). As one might expect, given their attitude to other providential gifts, once they have received Christianity the Utopians proceed to explore its potential for further evolution—in a way that is remarkably prophetic of issues that would arise during the Reformation and thereafter. For example, they dispute warmly as to whether it is really necessary for the sacraments to be administered only by a priest who has been ordained by a Christian bishop, rather than by someone chosen from their own number (219/16–19). They also make provision for priests to marry and for women to be chosen as priests (227/10–14, 229/19–22). In all this, quite apart from showing themselves to be proto-Lutheran reformers (which More must have been horrified to realize a few years later when he found himself obliged to refute some of these very practices after Luther had espoused them), the Utopians demonstrate their readiness to respond to the leadings of divine providence in whatever way God intends.

A major implication underlies More's vision of Utopia's religious attitudes. The society's experience suggests that the best state is one that provides the conditions in which human beings can most fully respond to the leadings of providence, and one that promotes the moral and religious attitudes that will induce them to do so. These are precisely the suggestions that More tries to develop throughout the section on Utopian religion.

The essential requirement for such favorable circumstances is religious liberty, and More's imaginative exemplum shows why. Significantly, the evolution of religious belief in Utopia is shown to be both historical and ahistorical. It is historical in the sense that when King Utopus first conquered the country the Utopians were wholly riven by interminable squabbles between competing superstitious sects, whereas they have subsequently been gradually moving toward a consensus of belief. The process whereby this happens has occupied all of their recorded history and is still continuing at the time when Hythlodaeus visits Utopia (219/37–38). The evolution of belief is ahistorical in that not all of the inhabitants are drawn to unite in "the one religion that seems more reasonable than the rest" at the same rate or at the same time. When Hythlodaeus visits the island, even though the majority of citizens have opted for the most common belief, many of them still worship different objects superstitiously as the embodiment of the divine power. The Utopians are thus shown to be in a continuous state of process that is relative for different people, but purposeful in terms of the common good nevertheless. As Hythlodaeus later puts it, "they are like travelers going to a single destination by different roads."3

The provisions that the Utopians have made for religious toleration implicitly acknowledge this. From the moment King Utopus conquered the island, he decreed that every man was free to cultivate the religion of his choice and seek to persuade others to it, provided that he did not engage in polemic (221/2–8). Utopus instituted this policy not merely for the sake of peace but to provide the best conditions for creative religious speculation:

> On religion he did not venture rashly to dogmatize. He was uncertain whether God did not desire a varied and manifold worship and therefore did not inspire different people with different views. But he was certain in thinking it both insolence and folly to demand by violence and threats that all should think to be true what you believe to be true. Moreover, even if it should be the case that one single religion is true and all the rest are false, he foresaw that, provided the matter was handled reasonably and moderately, truth by its own natural force would finally emerge sooner or later and stand forth conspicuously. (221/13–23)

Some critics, like Chambers and Surtz, have argued that the view More expresses here is one that he felt was appropriate to pagans only, and not to Christians, given that the latter had received the benefit of divine revelation, whereas the former had not. But there is no evidence in the text of *Utopia* that in 1515 More meant anything other than what he appears to say. Had he seriously believed that Christian belief had arrived at a definitive and final formulation, he would hardly have allowed the Utopians to speculate on its further evolution. Given that many of the questions the Utopians consider—such as whether priests can marry, women be made priests, or priests be ordained without a bishop—were topical issues at the time when More wrote the work, he would simply have been a seditious mischief-maker to raise them publicly had he not considered that there was some merit in allowing them to be discussed. However much he may have retreated from this utopian attitude later in his career when Lutheran extremism forced him into a reactionary stance, at the time when he wrote *Utopia* More meant everything he said.

One reason that we can be sure of this is that the Utopians' view of religious understanding is very similar to the view that More himself expresses concerning the evolution of Christian belief and practices in the earlier of his religious controversies, before his attitude hardened. In *A Dialogue Concerning Heresies*, for example, he could still declare that God reveals truth by degrees, disclosing more and more things "as it shall lyke his hygh goodnes and wysdome to dyspence and dyspose."[4] He could declare further that "things to be done" may be subject to historical change, "for in dyuerse tymes, dyuerse thynges may be conuenyent / and dyuerse maners of doynge" (*CW8*, pt. 2, 923/13–14). Certain mysteries, he could claim, are not disclosed "tyll the tymys appoyntyd by goddys hye prouydence mete and conuenyent for them," and when that time occurs, God "dothe insinuate and inspyre them into the brestys of his crysten people / that by the secrete instyncte of the holy gost they consent and agre togyther in one" (*CW6*, 146/17–24). This is precisely the process that More shows taking place among the Utopians. They are gradually uniting "in that one religion which seems to surpass the rest in reasonableness," thus confirming the providential nature of the experience of religious variety that they have been allowed to enjoy, and even their responsiveness to Christianity, More tells us, may be due to "the secret inspiration of God" (*secretius inspirante deo*) (217/28–29, 219/2–3). Utopian religious experience, therefore, is not essentially different to that which More would attribute to the Christian Church itself.

The Utopians' attitude toward religion is important within the exemplum as a whole, because it provides a corrective to the rational absolutism that they display in other areas of their communal life. In the ethical and social spheres, they constantly try to implement policies that embody the dictates of absolute reason, as, for example, when they declare that marriage is inviolable, that war is an activity fit only for beasts, or that pleasure is the supreme happiness (187/37–38, 199/36, 161/25–29). In all such cases when they invoke absolute principles, their experience eventually shows them that the definitive nature of their rational assumptions must be modified. They are forced to allow divorce on a proliferating number of grounds; they allow themselves to be drawn into wars that turn them into beasts indeed; and they come to concede that some practices springing from religious devotion are justifiable in terms that transcend those which reason alone can supply.

Their religious faith, in fact, leads the Utopians to condone practices their philosophy should prohibit. Within their society there exists a class of people devoted to good works, like European monks, called Buthrescae (meaning "extraordinarily religious"). These people divide into two sects: one that rejects all pleasures of this life and practices celibacy and the other that avoids no pleasure and extols marriage as a civic duty and a source of personal comfort (227/4–16). Confronted by the coexistence of these incompatible viewpoints, the Utopians concede the relative validity of both: "The Utopians regard [the second sort] as the wiser but the first-named as the holier. If the latter based upon arguments from reason their preference of celibacy to matrimony and of a hard life to a comfortable one, they would laugh them to scorn. Now, however, since they say they are prompted by religion, they look up to and reverence them. For there is nothing about which they are more careful than not lightly to dogmatize on any point of religion" (227/16–23).[5] Whereas, at the level of philosophical speculation, reason leads the Utopians to conclude that it is extreme madness "to exhaust the body by fasts, to injure one's health, and to reject all the other favors of nature" (177/39–179/2), at the level of religious faith they can accept that such actions may be purposeful in terms that reason alone may not be adequate to explain.

This readiness to allow faith to cooperate with reason, and so to modify some of the initial conclusions of reason, reveals the Utopians responsiveness to the leadings of providence. It manifests itself again in the way they modify their attitude toward pain. At the level of their philosophical discourse, the Utopians conclude that, because happiness resides in pleasure and because health is above all things conducive to pleasure, then pain and disease must be the bitter enemies of both health and pleasure (175/9–12). Consequently, they urge anyone who is suffering a disease that is not only incurable but also distressing and agonizing to free themselves "from this bitter life as from prison and the rack," by committing suicide (187/2–17). At the level of their religious discourse, however, especially that which is expressed as prayer, the Utopian attitude is different. Each citizen, instead of presuming to take on himself or herself the decision of when to die, is content to leave it to God: "how soon or late he does not venture to determine." And although Utopians pray that they may be accorded an easy death, they are prepared to suffer even "the hardest possible death" (*difficillima morte*), should God so require it as the means by which they come to him (237/27–32). Once again, therefore, the Utopians have allowed for a complete reversal of their attitude under the influence of providential inspiration.

More's aim throughout this concluding section of book 2 has been to show that the Utopians are able to resist any negative possibilities inherent in their utopianism because, at the level of faith, they maintain their trust in providence. To emphasize this further, More translates their faith into the petitions of their common prayer, placing the prayer itself at the structural climax of the exemplum. Each Utopian, Hythlodaeus tells us, may apply to himself personally what all recite together:

> In these prayers every man recognizes God to be the author of creation and governance and all other blessings besides. He thanks Him for all the benefits received, particularly that by the divine favor he has chanced on that commonwealth which is the happiest and has received that religion which he hopes to be the truest. *If* he errs in these matters or *if there is* anything better and more approved by God than that commonwealth or that religion, he prays that He will, of His goodness, bring him to the knowledge of it, for he is ready to follow in whatever path He may lead him. *But if* this form of a commonwealth be the best and his religion the truest, he prays that then He may give him steadfastness and bring all other mortals to the same way of living and the same opinion of God—*unless there be* something in this variety of religions which delights His inscrutable will. (237/12–26; my italics)

This prayer is noteworthy for the number of its conditional clauses. While on one hand the prayer affirms confidence in the merit of the polity and religion that the Utopians have attained in the present, the conditionals equally allow for the possibility that in the future the nature of what is desirable might change. Furthermore, the prayer assists the Utopians to work themselves into the positive state of mind that best prepares them for following wherever God might choose to lead them. The Utopians thus acknowledge that their institutions are instrumentally good, rather than definitively good, and commit themselves faithfully to the historical process in which providence invites them to participate.

This, one feels, is what More had come to believe constituted the true *optimo reipublicae statu* ("best state of a commonwealth") of the book's title. His ideal commonwealth existed not so much in a set of perfected institutions as in a communal state of mind capable of ensuring that a society's response to changing historical circumstances would be creative rather than destructive. He had come to see that "Utopia" truly was everywhere and nowhere—everywhere in that any society that aimed at ordering its institutions for the common good was reproducing the "utopian" condition of mind, and nowhere in that the imagined state of ideal perfection was unlikely ever to be attained on this earth. A society's willingness to keep on striving toward whatever elusive ideal it conceived of, More had concluded, was just as important as any actual results this effort might produce.

PROVIDENTIAL IMPERFECTIBILITY

More, in fact, had begun to formulate the view of the human situation that he would later expound systematically in his religious controversies. The various ironies and frustrations that the Utopians encounter in their effort to create a perfectly rational social order attest to the inherent imperfectibility of the world. Later More would argue that God had not created the world "to the vtterest poynt of souerayne goodness / that his almyghty maiestye coulde haue made it of," because "he wrought it not naturally but wyllyngly" for a special purpose. Indeed, God had contrived it to have "suche degrees of goodnes as his hye plesure lyked to lymyt," so that the very imperfections of the world, including human evil, might serve as the means by which God induces regenerative effort in people through the influence of the Holy Spirit (*CW6*, 74/32–75/2). Given God's providential plan to use human evil and other kinds of tribulation as an instrument for promoting goodness, it followed that no earthly society could ever be absolutely perfected. Rather, human life was conditioned by a "meruailouse straunge turning," as the devil seeks to pervert people through sensuality to sin and damnation, while God seeks to draw them back to obedience and salvation through reason and faith. More concluded that this dynamic process "neuer ceaseth nor neuer shall whyle thys world endureth" (*CW8*, pt. 2, 1020/28–33).

What More had established in the course of inventing Utopia was an implicit analogy between his ideal commonwealth and the Christian Church as he would soon describe it. Both the Utopian commonweal and the Church have founders, Utopus and Christ, who leave their followers fundamental beliefs and who establish institutions that are to be cultivated and developed through history. Both trust that divine providence will lead them gradually toward truth. But both are also in a militant state. More came to believe that the Church militant on earth is undergoing the process by which God is washing out her spots and wrinkles in preparation for her entry into "the pleasaunt weddyng chambre to the bed of eternall rest." This consummation, however, would only take place after the Last Judgment. In the meantime, "as faste as her husbande wassheth she spotteth, and as faste as he streccheth she wryncleth" (*CW6*, 206/1–3; cf. *CW8*, pt. 2, 865/28–32). In book 2 of *Utopia* More shows much the same kind of thing happening: as fast as the Utopians attempt to translate an ideal principle into action, the human situation just as quickly frustrates the attempt because of its inbuilt imperfection. It is the *process* involved in the attempt that is most important, not any specific conception of the ideal of perfection that motivates the attempt.

By the time he had finished writing book 2 of *Utopia*, therefore, More had resolved many of the questions on his mind, possibly in a way he had not anticipated when he began to write his *libellus*. He now knew that the reformist aspirations of his humanist colleagues were doomed to produce results that would inevitably fall short of their utopian expectations but that the attempt at reform must be made nonetheless. His problem now was to work out the implications of these insights for his own future career. Once again he chose to explore his options by dramatizing them in yet another fiction, as the dialogue that constitutes book 1 of *Utopia*. By appending it to the traveler's tale he had just penned, he vastly complicated the interpretation of an already complicated work.

8

More's Dilemma: The Context and Argument of Book 1

As I have argued, More appears to have been strongly drawn to a social ideal based on the notion of common ownership of property and wealth when he began to compose book 2 of *Utopia*. During the course of inventing his exemplum, however, he allowed insights to surface that threatened to subvert the ideal. Writing more as a poet than a theorizing philosopher, More was attempting to give his theoretical ideal a material embodiment, in much the way Duke Theseus describes in Shakespeare's *A Midsummer Night's Dream*:

> . . . as imagination bodies forth
> The forms of things unknown, the poet's pen
> Turns them to shapes, and gives to airy nothing
> A local habitation and a name.[1]

More faced the problem that, in order to give his visionary ideal a local habitation and name, he needed to clothe it in the trappings of real experience. This required him, in turn, fully to imagine the humane context in which such an ideal would have to operate. It was at this level that his idealism suffered a check.

The theoretical model did not account for two things: the perversity of human nature and the inherent irony of a human situation in which the outcome of human actions does not always accord with intentions. The ironies depicted in Utopian experience confirm that More had reached conclusions similar to those that another Shakespearean character would express: "Our wills and fates do so contrary run / That our devices still are overthrown; / Our thoughts are ours, their ends none of our own."[2] This is what the Utopians discover when, for example, their intervention into the quarrel between the Nephelogetes and the Alaopolitans causes a greater injustice than that which it is meant to remedy. In short, More's attempt at translating the theoretical ideal into an imagined reality had left him with doubts about the viability of the ideal, without entirely removing his faith in it.

Despite developing these doubts, More had nevertheless also identified a very positive aspect to the Utopians' political endeavor. Even though their effort to enshrine ideal principles in definitive institutions might be doomed to failure, there was something ennobling and regenerative in the effort itself. Moreover, the Utopians' history showed that great advances could be achieved in time through the cultivation of wisely founded institutions. More therefore found himself pulled two ways at once: his negative insights into utopianism fueled in him a degree of skepticism concerning humanist reforms aims, while his equally compelling insights into the necessity for the reformist effort drew him toward participating in it. Having thus acquired a viewpoint that was thoroughly paradoxical and deeply ambivalent, More had to work out what it all meant for him.

More and the Problem of Counsel

His problem was further compounded by a difficult career choice. As he explained to Erasmus in a letter written on his return to England in January 1516, Henry VIII had offered him an annuity to join the royal service (*Erasmus*, 3, no. 388, 234–35). More had demonstrated his effectiveness as a lawyer and undersheriff in the City of London, serving on several royal commissions of the peace and representing the interests of the London merchants. He had also, as William Roper tells us, recently defended the pope's interests successfully against the king in a law case involving an impounded ship, and Henry may have felt it wise to have such an effective advocate on his side rather than on anyone else's (Roper,

9–11). On top of that, More had acquired a high international profile as a humanist man of letters, and Henry, like his father before him, appreciated the advantage of having learned men on his payroll who could be used to celebrate the achievements of his dynasty and, as the occasion required, to assert the royal position in print. For whatever reason, More found that the king was putting pressure on him to enter the royal service.

This situation presented More with an acute dilemma. On the one hand, he, like other humanists, followed Cicero in believing that the learned man had a moral duty to work toward the common good by participating in public affairs. On the other hand, he could see the factors that would limit the effectiveness of such participation. The difficulty More experienced in making his decision is suggested by the length of time he took before accepting the king's offer, and the even longer time he took before he could bring himself to tell his friend Erasmus about it. Although he received the offer sometime between November 1515 and January 1516, he refused at first to accept it. Not until 26 August 1517, well over a year later, do we get conclusive evidence that More had been sworn in as a councillor, in a Commission for Calais that refers to him as acting in that capacity.[3]

Why did More delay so long? The reasons he gave Erasmus were convincing enough in themselves, but not fully candid: reluctance to abandon his position in the City of London (which was much more lucrative than the annuity he would receive) and his fear that his reputation would be compromised with the London citizens (*Erasmus*, 3, no. 388, 234–35). His real reasons lay deeper: he feared that his participation in court politics would be both futile and dangerous.

Even if book 1 of *Utopia* did not exist to confirm it, we can gauge something of what was in More's mind at this time by looking at several of his *Epigrams*, which were published with a later edition of *Utopia* in March of 1518. One of them, "*Quis optimus reipublicae status*" ("What Is the Best Form of Governing a Commonwealth"), closely echoes the title page of *Utopia*: *De optimo reipublicae statu deque noua insula Utopia* (*The Best State of a Commonwealth and the New Island of Utopia*). In this epigram More argues that a senate is preferable to a monarchy on the grounds that the former is less susceptible to abuse. But having argued this,

More arrests himself: "—but say, what started you on this inquiry anyway? Is there anywhere a people upon whom you yourself, by your own decision, can impose either a king or a senate? If this does lie within your power, you are king. Stop considering to whom you may give power. *The more basic question is whether it would do any good if you could.*"⁴ Whereas the body of the epigram reflects More's serious concern with finding out the best form of a commonwealth, the last part admits his doubt as to whether there is any real point in trying to do so. The final sentence shows him posing exactly the same question that the fictive representation of the Utopian commonwealth implies, and it is loaded with a pessimism that suggests the skeptical answer that More feared might need to be made.

A second epigram, "*Ad aulicum*" ("To a Courtier"), reveals a further cause of his reticence: "You often boast to me that you have the king's ear. . . . The real pleasure you get is not safe enough to relieve you of anxiety. For you it is a great pleasure. As for me, let my pleasure be less great—and safe" (*CW3*, pt. 2, 205, no. 162). More had a genuine fear that participation in court politics would jeopardize his personal safety. As he would say in book 1 of *Utopia*, "At court there is no room for dissembling, nor may one shut one's eyes to things. One must openly approve the worst counsels and subscribe to the most ruinous decrees. He would be counted a spy and almost a traitor, who gives only faint praise to evil counsels" (103/5–8). More was under no illusions as to the danger he might be putting himself into by joining the king's council, and, tragically, time would prove his fears to be well justified.

The sentiments More expresses in the *Epigrams*, considered in conjunction with the subject matter of book 1, help to explain the book's function, especially once the date of composition is ascertained. Erasmus reported to Ulrich von Hutten that More wrote book 1 after his return to England in late October 1515 (*Erasmus*, 7, no. 999, 24/282–83), and other evidence suggests that he had written at least two-thirds of it by late January 1516. In his account of an imaginary interview in the French king's council, Hythlodaeus refers to Ferdinand, King of Aragon, as if the latter were still alive, whereas Ferdinand died on 23 January 1516 (Hexter, *CW4*, xxxvi). Book 1 of *Utopia* was written, therefore, precisely during the time when More was considering the king's offer, and we can further surmise that he had been writing book 1 during the preceding couple of months as a means of objectifying his dilemma for the purpose of resolving it.

More did so by projecting his concerns into a fictive dialogue between two characters who represent his own divided impulses, and by then having them enter into an argument as to whether a wise man should or should not participate in politics. Hythlodaeus represents More's idealism and wisdom, while "More" represents his realism and prudence. Hythlodaeus embodies not only More's awareness of what he could contribute to the reform of English polity but also his instinct to withdraw from the attempt because of a fear of failure. "More" embodies his skepticism but also shows how that skepticism promotes an urge to participate in the hope of making things less bad than they might otherwise become. The relationship between these two characters is not one of simple antithesis, however, for the respective attitudes motivating them support a response in each that one would suppose should spring from the attitude of the other. Hythlodaeus's idealistic optimism—the view that society can be radically reformed—paradoxically supports an extreme form of pessimistic withdrawal, while "More's" skeptical pessimism—based on a belief that human nature is irremediably imperfect—motivates a comparatively optimistic attempt to ameliorate the worst effects of that imperfection. The perspective from which each character is viewed, therefore, is capable of turning itself inside out before one's very eyes, like Erasmus's Silenus in *The Praise of Folly*, so that everything becomes the opposite of what it seems, making the relationship between the two characters thoroughly ambiguous and paradoxical and a resolution of the conflict between their competing viewpoints well-nigh impossible.

THE CHARACTERIZATION OF HYTHLODAEUS AND "MORE"

At first More seems to have wanted to develop an extreme contrast between Hythlodaeus and "More." When we first see Hythlodaeus, he is described as "a man of advanced years, with sunburnt countenance and long beard and cloak hanging carelessly from his shoulder, while his appearance and dress seemed . . . to be those of a ship's captain (49/17–23). These details of his physical appearance signal the most salient facts about him. His likeness to a ship's captain and his sunburnt complexion warn us that he is a traveler, and we are soon told that "his sailing has not been like that of Palinurus but that of Ulysses or, rather, of Plato" (49/36–37). In other words, Hythlodaeus is a speculative mental traveler, as well as a literal traveler of great experience. In order to free himself for such travel, Hythlodaeus has cast off all family responsibilities. He has left his patrimony to his brothers, and disclaims any obligation to help them further:

> "As for my relatives and friends," he replied, "I am not greatly troubled about them, for I think I have fairly well performed my duty to them already. The possessions, which other men do not resign unless they are old and sick and even then resign unwillingly when incapable of retention, I divided among my relatives and friends when I was not merely hale and hearty but actually young. I think they ought to be satisfied with this generosity from me and not to require or expect additionally that I should, for their sakes, enter into servitude to kings." (55/23–31)

Hythlodaeus's disheveled appearance equally implies his indifference to worldly considerations. His unkempt beard and carelessly arranged cloak suggest a lack of concern with making the favorable impression that is necessary for a courtier to gain the confidence of a king, and hence is symptomatic of the attitude that largely disqualifies him from effective participation in political life.

"More," on the other hand, is shown as being deeply concerned with all these things. When book 1 opens, he is depicted as already in the service of a king, having been sent as an emissary of Henry VIII to settle an economic dispute between his master and the future emperor, Charles V. This activity represents the "servitude" of which Hythlodaeus complains, particularly as the negotiations are shown to have reached a frustrating stalemate. Unlike Hythlodaeus, he is also depicted as homesick for his family, which is why he finds the company of the Belgian humanist, Peter Giles, so congenial: "His delightful society and charming discourse largely took away my nostalgia and made me less conscious than before of the separation from my home, wife, and children to whom I was exceedingly anxious to get back, for I had then been more than four months away" (49/12–16). Whereas Hythlodaeus's main interest is philosophy, or the *vita contemplativa*, "More's" energies are shown to be totally absorbed by the active life, or *vita activa*, as he declares in his prefatory letter to Giles: "I am constantly engaged in legal business, either pleading or hearing, either giving an award as arbiter or deciding a case as judge. I pay a visit of courtesy to one man and go on business to another. I devote almost the whole day in public to other men's affairs and the remainder to my own. I leave to myself, that is to learning, nothing at all" (39/27–33). It is little wonder, then, that being committed to such different life-styles and responsibilities, the two characters should espouse radically different political philosophies and advocate divergent modes of political action: Hythlodaeus can afford to, "More" cannot.

Part of More's point in developing this contrast is to show that the choice with which he was confronted also involved a choice between conflicting life-styles. He can hardly have been unaware that his friend Erasmus, a bachelor, was enjoying a Hythlodaean freedom from which he himself was excluded by his married circumstances. Perhaps he was also suggesting that the way different people respond to the problem of political action is conditioned by the self-interested, subjective perspectives that their chosen life-styles necessitate. Whatever his motive, he shows in the very full characterization of his two main protagonists that more is involved in the kind of choice he was required to make in real life than philosophical idealism alone.

Ironically, this putative contrast between Hythlodaeus and "More" rapidly threatens to collapse into an equation as the two characters encounter a common problem: how to reconcile what is right with what is expedient. Cicero, in expounding his view of a wise man's duty, had encountered exactly the same problem. In *De officiis* (*On Moral Obligation*), a work *Utopia* constantly echoes, Cicero declares that the only valid excuses for not participating in public affairs are ill-health, or when men of extraordinary genius devote themselves to learning. He certainly did not approve of those who withdraw because "they seem to dread the toil and trouble and also, perhaps, the discredit and humiliation of political failure and defeat."[5] The philosopher should feel protected by a certain truth inherent in the nature of things: "that if anything is morally right, it is expedient, and if anything is not morally right, it is not expedient" (De officiis, 3.3.11). Even Cicero, however, was forced to admit that it sometimes happens "that what is accustomed under ordinary circumstances to be considered morally wrong is found not to be morally wrong," and that this "may sometimes give room for a doubt and seem to call for consideration" (De officiis, 3.4.19). In the argument that More develops between Hythlodaeus and "More" this issue becomes a consideration with a vengeance.

When it is proposed to Hythlodaeus that a man of his experience and wisdom should enter the service of a king, he reacts violently against the idea, citing as his reason the fact that kings prefer war to peace, and that royal councilors, being filled with ridiculous and obstinate prejudices, are unwilling to profit by wise counsel (55/15-59/17). He thus identifies two of the main causes for conflict between what is morally right and what is expedient in political situations. To illustrate his point, he recounts several anecdotes—the first dealing with an actual experience he had in England and the second with an imaginary interview in the French king's council.

The first anecdote concerns a visit Hythlodaeus made to the household of Cardinal John Morton, More's former patron and at that time lord chancellor under King Henry VII. While dining at Morton's table, Hythlodaeus declares, he had occasion to comment on the huge numbers of thieves being hanged in England and on the injustice of hanging as a punishment for simple theft. As a more equitable alternative he proposes a modified Roman system of penal servitude, in which the aim of the punishment is to destroy vices and save men instead of killing them (75/16-79/37). The importance of this first anecdote is that it gives More a pretext for offering his own analysis of the causes of contemporary social ills in England and for showing how useful he could be, at least potentially, in providing imaginative remedies.

Both in his analysis and the remedies he proposes, Hythlodaeus appears to have logic and morality on his side. He points out that people can hardly be blamed for thieving if they are the victims of penury that is not their fault. He identifies a number of social and economic factors in early Tudor England that were forcing men to steal. Foreign and civil wars were leaving men crippled, so that they could no longer work. The retainers of noblemen were often turned out without any knowledge of a trade by which they could earn their living. Enclosure of arable land for the raising of sheep was leading to the eviction of tenant farmers and to higher prices for food and other commodities. Meanwhile, the inappropriate luxury and ostentatious display of the rich was furnishing a perpetual source of provocation and temptation to thievery (61/35–69/37).

Hythlodaeus believes that the situation in England can be remedied by a resumption of arable farming and cloth-making to provide more jobs, the restriction of monopolies to keep down prices, and, above all, by a more equitable system for dealing with theft. Instead of being put to death, he proposes, thieves should be made to make restitution to the owner of the stolen goods and forced to undertake constructive hard labor, with the prospect of eventual liberty as a reward for good conduct (75/24–79/37).

There is only one problem with this kind of reasoning, Hythlodaeus finds: no one seems prepared to listen to it. An English lawyer who is present at Morton's table simply buries Hythlodaeus's main points under a load of obfuscating legal verbiage (71/18–30), while a parasite who liked to play the fool destroys the chance of Hythlodaeus's proposals being taken seriously when he uses them to make a joke at the expense of an irascible friar. When the friar reacts with vehement indignation the whole dinner party is disrupted and the moment for serious reflection lost (81/26–85/26).

Hythlodaeus's frustration is even more intense when he imagines trying to propose wise laws to some king and to uproot from this king's soul the seeds of evil and corruption. To illustrate his point, he visualizes himself in the French king's council, arguing against various immoral schemes to extend French dominion and raise excessive revenue. To counter the first, he imagines himself proposing the example of the Achorians, who force their king to choose one kingdom and one only (89/31–91/20). Then, to counter the second, he imagines himself proposing the example of the Macarians, who make their king swear a solemn oath that he will never have in his treasury at any one time more than a thousand pounds of gold, or its equivalent in silver (97/16–35).

What these experiences, real and imaginary, prove to Hythlodaeus is that corruption is so rife in politics, and human nature so perverse, that philosophy has no place at all in the councils of kings. To put it in Ciceronian terms, Hythlodaeus believes that what is morally right will always take second place to what is politically expedient. Furthermore, he departs from Cicero in believing that a yawning gulf often exists between the two, rather than the identity that Cicero tried to allege. Consequently, Hythlodaeus has become thoroughly disillusioned, and his response is to remain detached from political involvement.

"More," who is already committed to the active life, is forced to concede the truth of much of what Hythlodaeus says, but his own response is very different. Instead of withdrawal from politics, he advocates accommodating one's actions to a particular situation so as to make a form of efficacious participation possible:

> If you cannot pluck up wrongheaded opinions by the root, if you cannot cure according to your heart's desire vices of long standing, yet you must not on that account desert the commonwealth. You must not abandon the ship in a storm because you cannot control the winds.
>
> On the other hand, you must not force upon people new and strange ideas which you realize will carry no weight with persons of opposite conviction. On the contrary, by the indirect approach you must seek and strive to the best of your power to handle matters tactfully. What you cannot turn to good you must make as little bad as you can. For it is impossible that all should be well unless all men were good, a situation which I do not expect for a great many years to come! (99/31 – 101/4)

In contrast to Hythlodaeus, "More" is prepared to accept that imperfection is ultimately irremediable, and that therefore the absolute nature of moral principles must give way to what is expedient for a particular time and place. Thus the two protagonists of book 1, although they try to grapple with the same problem, choose diametrically opposed responses to it. Between them, they encompass the alternatives that were available to More as he contemplated whether or not he should enter the service of Henry VIII.

MORE'S RELATION TO HIS CHARACTERS

Where did More himself actually stand in all this? On the evidence of book 1, it is impossible to tell, for More took pains to construct the fiction in such a way as to make it impossible for the reader to determine with any confidence whether the view of one character is being privileged over that of the other. The very names of the two protagonists are ambiguous. "Raphael" is the name of the archangel who is sent by God to look after Tobias and free his children and his wife, Sara, from the devil (Tobias 12:14 [Vulgate]). His name in Hebrew literally means "healer of God." The suggestions inherent in his Christian name, therefore, are all positive, implying his role as a divine messenger who is capable of offering a cure for the ills of a suffering Europe. These positive connotations are instantly canceled out by his surname, however, for "Hythlodaeus" means "speaker of nonsense." His surname intercepts the positive connotations inherent in his Christian name, threatening to substitute negative ones in their place.

A similar ambiguity arises from "More's" name. By giving "More" the name of his real-life creator, More might appear to be investing the views of the former with an unequivocal authorial sanction. But the Latin *morus* literally means "fool," and we are not given enough information to decide whether "More" is the stupid fool Hythlodaeus thinks he is or whether the pun in his name ironically emphasizes the gap between the folly it denotes and the actual wisdom "More" possesses.

To compound the effect of these ambiguous signals, More shows that Hythlodaeus is an unreliable narrator in that he is unable to detect as much meaning in the events he witnesses as the reader is induced to see in them. The episode at Morton's table is a case in point. Hythlodaeus tells the story to prove his contention that courtiers would pay him little attention were he to enter the world of politics. He cannot see that the anecdote could be used to prove the very opposite of what he thinks it does. We see, as Hythlodaeus does not, that he is predisposed to register primarily the skepticism and scoffing of the sycophantic parasites that hang around Morton. He seems to have overlooked the significance of the cardinal's reaction to his plan for replacing hanging with penal servitude as the punishment for thievery. Morton cautiously approves it, being prepared to implement it on a trial basis, and on his own initiative suggests that it might be extended to vagrants as well as thieves (81/7–18). Given that Morton, as lord chancellor, is in a position to effect policy, Hythlodaeus has demonstrated the opportunity available to philosophers to influence things for the better, only he does not know he has. Perhaps it is this blindness in Hythlodaeus that moved Peter Giles to express his belief to Busleyden that "in all the five years which Raphael spent on the island, he did not see as much as one may perceive in More's description" (23/5–7).

"More," too, is shown to have blind spots of his own. In his prefatory letter to Giles, he confesses that he does "not entirely distrust" himself to have forgotten nothing of what he was told and admits that he does not even know where the island of Utopia is (41/14–43/5). Such admissions are symptomatic of a certain prevarication that "More" displays throughout the work. Hence if Hythlodaeus may seem excessively convinced of his own rightness, "More" may in his turn strike some readers as excessively diffident.

The two characters, indeed, threaten to cancel each other out by subverting the foundations of each other's position. When "More" proposes his policy of accommodation and oblique action, Hythlodaeus denounces it scornfully on the grounds that, by the same argument, one would need to dissemble the Commandments when Christ Himself forbad such dissembling. Such a course of action, Hythlodaeus declares, would merely make it easier for men to be bad in greater comfort (101/23–36). "More" has no answer to these objections to his "civil philosophy" and simply lapses into silence. Hythlodaeus, on the other hand, is equally guilty of such evasion when More objects to his view that the abolition of money and property is the precondition for a commonwealth to have justice and prosperity. Toward the end of book 1 Hythlodaeus espouses communism as a radical solution to the problem of reconciling moral right with expedient political action. It is his way of cutting through the Gordian knot the fiction has exposed. Predictably, "More" will have nothing to do with such a definitive solution and voices objections similar to those Aristotle made in his critique of Plato's *Republic*.

Life cannot be satisfactory where all things are common. How can there be a sufficient supply of goods when each withdraws himself from the labor of production? For the individual does not have the motive of personal gain and he is rendered slothful by trusting to the industry of others. Moreover, when people are goaded by want and yet the individual cannot legally keep as his own what he has gained, must there not be trouble from continual bloodshed and riot? This holds true especially since the authority of magistrates and respect for their office have been eliminated, for how there can be any place for these among men who are all on the same level I cannot even conceive. (107/5–16)

Just as "More" had no answer to Hythlodaeus's denunciation of the moral hypocrisy that the "civil philosophy" required, so too does Hythlodaeus have no immediate answer to "More's" skeptical common sense. He merely appeals to the example of Utopia to prove his case:

"I do not wonder," he rejoined, "that it looks this way to you, being a person who has no picture at all, or else a false one, of the situation I mean. But you should have been with me in Utopia and personally seen their manners and customs as I did. . . . In that case you unabashedly would admit that you had never seen a well-ordered people anywhere but there." (107/17–23)

By shifting the argument from one grounded in theory to one derived empirically from actual experience, Hythlodaeus has deftly indulged in a classic form of evasion. The problem with such a tactic is that it makes the burden of proof rest with the Utopian exemplum, and, as we have seen, the fiction of book 2, like life itself, is susceptible to different interpretations according to the onlooker's dispositions.

One suspects that More could not allow either of his surrogates to gain unequivocal ascendancy over the other because each was expressing perceptions that he had come to acknowledge as valid. Between them, in fact, Hythlodaeus and "More" reproduce the experience of the Utopians themselves. Hythlodaeus shares the Utopians' inability to square absolute moral principles with the practicalities of social and political life. He also displays a comparable response to the frustration of his idealism. Just as the Utopians react vehemently against those who resist the logic or justice of the policies they try to apply, Hythlodaeus reacts to More's objections with a sharpness and sarcasm that most people would find highly offensive (101/30–35). Conversely, the "civil philosophy" "More" advocates depends on the same kind of assumption that motivates the Utopians' religious faith: that there is something purposeful and creative about attempting to grapple with imperfection, even though a perfect remedy for it might never be found. In real life, More found that he needed to alternate between acting the role of "More" and that of Hythlodaeus, finding each mode of action to have validity in its own terms according to the circumstances. This explains why neither one is privileged over the other in book 1. More had attained perceptions that were far too multivalent for him to be able to take an unequivocal stand.

The ironies worked into the fiction of book 1 thus take us back eventually to the point where we started—with the ambivalence generated by book 2. By the time he had finished writing book 1 More had fully explored his dilemma without actually resolving it. There were only two courses left to him: either to abort the whole enterprise and withhold the publication of *Utopia* (which he seems from time to time to have been tempted to do) or to find some way of making his unresolved dilemma purposeful for the book's subsequent readers. While he was tempted to opt for the first, he eventually chose the second course, and the way in which he did so is what I discuss in chapter 9.

9

"*Si quid sit in ambiguo*":
The Inconclusiveness of *Utopia*

By the time More finished book 1 of *Utopia* he was even further than before from resolving his dilemma. The imaginative exemplification of the theory to which he inclined, in book 2, had put the effectiveness of that theory in doubt, while the dialogue of book 1 had put even the effectiveness of political participation in doubt. More had discovered, in fact, that he had very equivocal feelings about some of the most fundamental axioms and aspirations of the humanist political philosophy to which he was most drawn.

Having allowed these feelings to rise to the surface of his consciousness in the displaced fictions he had created, More then was faced with a need to protect himself, first, against criticism and ridicule and, second, against his own awareness of how deeply he wished some of the things he had shown in the fiction to be true in fact. He achieved this protection by distancing himself progressively from his own creation. In the first instance he distanced himself from the Utopian exemplum by creating a narrator to describe it who, as we have seen, turns out to be unreliable. Once Hythlodaeus had been introduced—and there is no evidence that he existed in his creator's mind at the time when he first wrote the description of the Utopian commonwealth—it was no longer possible to assume that the political system described in book 2 necessarily had its author's assent, especially once there had been created a character named "More" who explicitly disagrees with much of what Hythlodaeus says. Then, having distanced himself from the exemplum, More proceeded to distance himself from both of his surrogates by juxtaposing their unresolved disagreement against the exemplum, thereby placing it in the position of having to carry the burden of proving one side or the other. The dialogue in book 1 is thus made to interrogate the exemplum in book 2, and vice versa, so that any fixed authorial viewpoint becomes impossible to determine, let alone serve as a stable norm. Finally, More distanced himself still further by allowing Erasmus and Peter Giles to supply the work with parerga and marginal glosses, and by soliciting commendatory letters from other humanists on the Continent. These additional items show a range of readers interpreting *Utopia* in various ways and place a screen between the reader and the work, and especially between the reader and the author. By the time *Utopia* was published More had made it impossible to detect where he really stood, which is not surprising, given that the letters preceding the work's publication show him to have vacillated in his attitude toward it.

THE EFFECT OF THE FRAMING DIALOGUE

It was a stroke of genius on More's part to enclose the exemplum of book 2 in the dialogue that commences in book 1, for the effect is to change the status of the exemplum altogether. The description of Utopia is delivered as an unbroken monologue designed specifically to extol the virtues of the Utopian commonweal. Had it remained simply a monologue, readers might justifiably have assumed that it contains a closed, determinate meaning endorsed by the author himself. As it is, the presence of the dialogue between Hythlodaeus and "More," wrapped around the exemplum, destroys the possibility of authorial closure in book 2. Dialogue is by its very nature "dialogical" (to use a current critical term), especially when it takes place between fully dramatized characters in a fully realized setting that sustains credibility as a convincing imitation of life—that is, the meaning remains open, rather than closed, with the reader being given far more scope to contribute to the process whereby meaning is generated. Not only is book 1 dialogical in its own terms, in that it refuses to present a resolution of the argument between its two main characters, but the addition of book 1 to book 2 also has the effect of making book 2 dialogical as well, since Hythlodaeus wants it to prove a proposition that "More" doubts can be proven, and it is left to the reader to decide which of them is right.

This effect is consolidated in the coda to the whole work. After Hythlodaeus has delivered an impassioned peroration in which he praises Utopia as the only just commonweal and delivers a sermon against the pride vitiating the social systems of other countries, "More" enters the fiction yet again to respond to Hythlodaeus:

> When Raphael had finished his story, many things came to my mind which seemed very absurdly established in the customs and laws of the people described—not only in their method of waging war, their ceremonies and religion, as well as their other institutions, but most of all in that feature which is the principal foundation of their whole structure. I mean their common life and subsistence—without any exchange of money. *This latter alone utterly overthrows all the nobility, magnificence, splendor, and majesty which are, in the estimation of the common people, the true glories and ornaments of the commonwealth.* (245/17–26; my italics)

By specifying the fundamental institution of common ownership as one of the aspects of Utopia he considers to be "very absurdly established," the authorial More effectively pulls the rug out from under any interpretative certainty on the part of the reader. The skillfulness of this move can be demonstrated with reference to the passage I have italicized. It would be a brave (or foolish) reader who declares that he or she knows who is being ironic here—More, or only "More."

The possibility remains open, indeed, that "More" (or More) seriously means what he says.[1] At the very least, this conclusion always remained latent in More's mind, ready to be activated as the occasion required. This is confirmed by certain statements in his later controversial writings. In *Responsio ad Lutherum* (1522), for instance, he rejected Luther's claim for evangelical liberty on the grounds that Luther's assumptions about human nature were very foolish: "As if even the best magistrates could manage either that the whole Christian people would want to live in common or that the wicked would not want to steal or that any preaching of the faith could procure that no one anywhere would be wicked."[2] This assertion would seem to pick up, and give credit to, the skepticism that "More" voiced in book 1 of *Utopia* when he declared that Hythlodaeus's desire to effect a radical transformation of society would be impossible unless all men were good—a situation he did not anticipate (101/2–3).

More reveals his skepticism about the viability of communal ownership even more explicitly in *A Dialogue of Comfort* (1534). In response to his nephew Vincent's scruples about men acquiring wealth when there are so many poor people in the world, More has Anthony reply,

> Verely Cosyn . . . syns Christes dayes to the worldes end . . . there hath neuer lakkyd pore men nor neuer shall. . . . [M]en of sub-staunce must there be / for els mo beggers shall you haue perdy then there be, & no man left able to releve an nother. For this I thinke in my mynd a very sure conclucion / that yf all the money that is in this countrey were to morow next brought to gether out of euery mans hand & laid all vppon one hepe, and that devidid among all / the best shuld be left litle bettre than than almost a beggar is now / And yet he that was a begger before, all that he shall be the richer for that he shuld therby receyve, shall not make hym mych above a beger still. . . . Men can not you wot well lyve here in this world, but yf that some one man prouide a meane of lyvyng for some other many. . . . For surely the rich mans substaunce is the well spring of the pore mans livyng.[3]

In the light of these later comments by More, therefore, it is unwise for any reader of *Utopia* to dismiss "More's" objections as merely rhetorical and ironic, even though the reader is invited to wonder whether they are being presented as being so.

Back in the coda to book 2 of *Utopia* More leaves open for readers the possibility of reaching one conclusion or the other: either Hythlodaeus's belief that the abolition of property is the mainspring of a just society or "More's" belief that such a system would leave the real problem (of human wickedness) essentially unaltered. Strategically, he deflects readers' attention to the way in which "More" treats Hythlodaeus at the end of his discourse, for his words and actions demonstrate the virtues of the "civil philosophy" in action. Bearing in mind that Hythlodaeus is likely to be wearied from the telling of his tale, and knowing from his earlier argument that Hythlodaeus does not readily brook any opposition to his views, "More" takes him by the hand and leads him in to dinner, postponing until a future occasion further consideration of the issues he has raised. Laconically, "More" adds, "If only this were some day possible!" (245, 35–36). The book concludes with "More" declaring that "there are very many features in the Utopian commonwealth which it is easier for me to wish for in our countries than to have any hope of seeing realized," an opinion with which very many readers are likely to concur (247/1–3).

The conclusion to book 2 serves another very important purpose as far as the reader is concerned. By anticipating that there will be a further occasion on which he will be able to reactivate debate on the matters Hythlodaeus has raised, "More"—and by extension More—has set up a need for the dialogue to be continued. Perhaps the consummate irony of the work is that this dialogue has been very vigorously pursued through four centuries and is still being vigorously pursued whenever an important election is held. It is reactivated, in fact, whenever someone reads the work, and especially when students (some of whom are likely to be future politicians) discuss it. The important thing to realize is that the ending of *Utopia* leaves all the issues More has raised unresolved and the debate open-ended. It is left to individual readers, in their own time and place, to resolve.

The inconclusiveness built into the fiction by the addition of book 1 to book 2 is neatly summed up in the title page of the original edition, which reads,

Libellus vere aureus nec minus salutaris quam festiuus de optimo reip. statu, deque noua Insula Utopia authore clarissimo viro Thoma Moro inclytae ciuitatis Londinensis ciue & vicecomite cura M. Petri Aegidii Antuerpiensis, & arte Theodorici Martini Alustensis, Typographi almae Louaniensium Academiae nunc primum accuratissime editus. (Gibson, 5)

(A truly golden little book, no less salutary than entertaining, on the best state of a commonwealth, and on the new island of Utopia, by the distinguished author Thomas More, a citizen and undersheriff of the famous city of London, under the care of Master Peter Giles of Antwerp, and by the skill of Thierry Martens of

Giles's letter to Busleyden further undermines the claim that is being made for Utopia's status as an ideal polity by raising doubts about Hythlodaeus' reliability as a narrator: "By heaven, I am even disposed to believe that in all the five years which Raphael spent on the island, he did not see as much as one may perceive in More's description" (23/5–7). Again, readers can feel that they are being invited to conclude that Utopia is even more marvelous than Hythlodaeus thinks it is, but they are just as free to suspect that Hythlodaeus might not have seen aspects of Utopia that could weaken the foundations of his argument. Significantly, Giles sustains More's facetiousness by reporting that neither he nor More know where Utopia is, because a servant distracted More's attention, and another member of the company happened to cough just at the moment when Hythlodaeus was telling of its geographical location (23/27–35). Giles's readiness to extend both the paradoxical irony and witty facetiousness that run through the work attests to the fact that he was far more "in the know" as far as More's authorial intentions were concerned than any of the other humanists who would comment on the work.

This becomes quite apparent when we consider the remaining prefatory items in the 1516 edition. John Desmarais of Cassel supplies a letter to Giles in which he claims of *Utopia*, without the faintest hint of irony, that "whatever pertains to the good constitution of a commonwealth may be seen in it as in a mirror," and then adds a poem proclaiming Utopia as "the total sum of all virtue once for all" (27/34–29/30). Likewise, Busleyden writes a letter to More in which he sees in Utopia "a description of the good and just constitution, which all must desire," a "pattern and perfect model of morality" that he urges as a model for Europe (33/15–37/27). Both the tone and sentiments of Desmarais and Busleyden contrast sharply with the equivocal irony with which Giles's contributions are imbued.

It is only when we get to More's own letter to Giles, described in the first edition as a *praefatio* (preface), that the irony returns. Under the pretext of excusing his style, More alludes to Hythlodaeus's "careless simplicity" that it purports to imitate. This may seem innocent enough, if one is inclined to accept it as such, but the phrase "careless simplicity" (*neglectam simplicitatem*) is capable of denoting a type of "negligence" and "simplicity" that are far less flattering if taken as referring to Hythlodaeus's usual habits of mind (39/13–14).

More also reintroduces the paradoxes that had appeared in Giles's parerga. In asking Giles to verify his account of the length of the bridge spanning the river Anydrus, he declares that he has put down what he himself *seems* to remember, so that even if it turns out to be untrue, he has not been dishonest: "(. . . thus, if there is anything ambiguous [in the account of Utopia], I would rather report a lie, than tell a lie, for I would sooner be honest than wise)" (40/28–29) (. . . *ita si quid sit in ambiguo, potius mendacium dicam, quam mentiar, quod malim bonus esse quam prudens*). This statement is very slippery indeed, for More gives the reader no firm guidance as to either the level of seriousness with which it is to be taken, or the things to which it might refer. By warning readers that he may be lying without necessarily being a liar, More is leaving all expressive opportunities open for himself as author, and all interpretative possibilities wide open for his readers. He is essentially emphasizing the relativity of perceptions of truth: people are imprisoned within the limits of their own vision of it—which is, by extension, just as true for Hythlodaeus, or the humanists who annotated the successive editions, or for us, as he is here claiming it is for him.

Finally, in his prefatory letter to Giles—after describing the reaction of a religious zealot who wishes to rush off to Utopia and hasten the conversion to Christianity of its inhabitants—More anticipates that his book will elicit a range of faulty responses on the part of people who are either peevish, ungrateful, wrongheaded, or self-indulgent (43/30–39).

The parerga of the 1516 edition, therefore, alternately nudge readers toward an unequivocal approbation of the Utopian commonwealth and then undermine their confidence in the soundness of the judgments they may have been feeling tempted to adopt. As a result, the highly equivocal and ambiguous perspective that is sustained in the fictive dialogue and exemplum of books 1 and 2 is extended beyond the confines of the fiction into the real world of the reader, with highly perplexing consequences.

It is interesting to see how the editor of the second edition of *Utopia*, which was printed in Paris in 1517, tried to iron out some of the perplexity. Just as he doctored the title page to lessen its ambiguity and playfulness, he also replaced some of the 1516 edition with new items in order to invest the work with a higher degree of seriousness. The map of Utopia, the Utopian alphabet, and the verses in the Utopian vernacular were omitted, possibly because the editor had no patience with fostering that kind of fictive verisimilitude, or because of the printer's reluctance to hire an artist to do the woodcuts. Anemolius's hexastichon, however, was included—presumably because of its eulogy of Utopia as a victor over Plato's *Republic*, and its final stress on Utopia as a Eutopia. The editor then reinforced this favorable impression by including a new letter, this time from Budé to Thomas Lupset, which unequivocally praises Utopian institutions as conforming to natural law and the principles of Christ (11/4–30). Budé's only concession to the ironic tenor of the work is to allow latitude for doubt as to whether the story can really be believed: "Now, the island of Utopia, which I hear is called also Udepotia, is said, by a singularly wonderful stroke of fortune (*if we are to believe the story*), to have adopted the customs and the true wisdom of Christianity" (11/4–6; my italics). "*If we are to believe Hythlodaeus*, she [Justice] must have remained behind on the island of Utopia and not yet have made her way to the sky" (11/39–13/2; my italics). Despite allowing this doubt and suggesting an alternative name for the island that emphasizes even more firmly its nonexistence (*Udepotia* means "Never-Land"), Budé's statements are not ironic in the same way that More's or Giles's are, nor do they have the same subversive effect. They simply serve to emphasize the outstanding novelty of such excellent institutions as the Utopians possess. The other additions to the 1517 edition—the eulogistic poems by Gerhard Geldenhauer and Cornelis de Schrijver—simply consolidate the serious impression that the editor wants the book to make on the reader. Geldenhauer praises both book and island as being consummately "pleasant" and "profitable," while de Schrijver praises it for uncovering the sources of all virtues and vices (31/1–19).

With the 1517 edition having pushed *Utopia* in the direction of an unequivocal, eulogistic interpretation, the third edition of 1518, this time overseen by Erasmus himself, takes the final logical step. Erasmus implies, with a rather patronizing condescension, that any inconsistencies or deficiencies in the work can be attributed to More's lack of a fully adequate humanist training: "What would this wonderful, rich nature not have accomplished if his talent had been trained in Italy, if it were now totally devoted to the service of the muses, if it had ripened to its proper harvest and, as it were, its own autumnal plenty?" (3/11–14). Erasmus brought all the Utopiana back in, but, one suspects, he did so for their ornamental rather than thematic value, since this edition, from the press of Froben, was a very lavish production indeed (see Gibson, 7–12).

Altogether, then, the parerga to *Utopia* depict a range of reactions, real and imaginary, that become incorporated into a larger mimesis in which the boundaries between fiction and reality begin to merge. These reactions, which often contain reports of other reactions, have the effect of a hall of mirrors, in which reflections are reflected within other reflections, until the object itself and its illusory image become impossible to distinguish. Moreover, the reactions are shown to range across the whole spectrum of interpretative possibilities. On the one hand, they seem to offer guidance for readers; on the other, they seem to deprive them of guidance, which is More's way of warning readers in advance that they would be foolish to pin his work down to any one definitive meaning but equally foolish to dismiss from consideration any of the interpretations the book has figured forth. Indeed, it is possible to hypothesize that the range of responses More allowed to be incorporated into his fiction reproduced many of the reactions he had already experienced himself in the course of exemplifying his idea. In terms of its overall representation, therefore, *Utopia* came to offer More both a catharsis and a corrective, as well as a disguise.

HOW MORE VIEWED THE PUBLICATION OF *UTOPIA*

One would expect that More had sufficiently covered his tracks to be able to publish *Utopia* with equanimity, but the letters he wrote immediately prior to, and after, its publication show this not to have been the case. These letters prove that his ambivalence toward his fictive commonwealth extended beyond the work's covers. At first sight, this ambivalence might appear to have sprung merely from More's sensitivity as an author to the prospect that *Utopia* might receive unfavorable criticism on account of defects in its style and presentation. On 3 September 1516 More wrote to inform Erasmus that he was sending him his *Nusquama* ("Nowhere"), "which is nowhere well written" (*Letters*, no. 6, 73). In another letter (20 September 1516) he tells Erasmus that he is "most anxious" that *Utopia* be published soon, and that it be "handsomely set off with the highest of recommendations" from notable people, because one individual has regretted that the book is being published before the lapse of nine years (*Letters*, no. 7, 76).

There is more to More's concern, however, than mere defensiveness about the work's style. He had invested a lot of emotional energy in the creation of *Utopia* and had very high hopes for it. That is why the approval of other distinguished humanists and statesmen was so important to him. Writing again to Erasmus on 31 October 1516 he declares that he is "very anxious" that *Utopia* meet with the approval of Tunstall, Busleyden, and John le Sauvage, adding, peculiarly, that this is more than he could wish for, "since they are so fortunate as to be top-ranking officials in their own governments" (*Letters*, no. 9, 80–81). One could almost infer from this that More was pinning his hopes on *Utopia* as the credentials that would qualify him to be a statesman like the others. When Tunstall had given his approval, More wrote not only to him to convey his delight that Tunstall's judgment was so favorable (*Letters*, no. 10, 82) but also to Erasmus to describe his exhilaration:

> You have no idea how thrilled I am; I feel so expanded, and I hold my head high. For in my daydreams I have been marked out by my Utopians to be their king forever; I can see myself now marching along, crowned with a diadem of wheat, very striking in my Franciscan frock, carrying a handful of wheat as my sacred scepter, thronged by a distinguished retinue of Amaurotians, and, with this huge entourage, giving audience to foreign ambassadors and sovereigns. (*Letters*, no. 11, 84–85)

This daydream perhaps reveals more clearly than anything else just how deeply attracted More was to his utopian vision. In half of his mind, the vision itself, like the just-described dream, was a displaced objectification not only of his latent ambition to become important as a statesmen but also of his sense of the kind of polity he would like to achieve and in which, as a statesman, he would like to serve. Nevertheless, there was another, more negative level in More's thinking at which his own vision ceased to carry conviction with him. It becomes visible even in the conclusion of his utopian daydream: "I was going to continue with this fascinating vision, but the rising Dawn has shattered my dream—poor me!—and shaken me off my throne and summons me back to the drudgery of the courts. But at least this thought gives me consolation: real kingdoms do not last much longer" (*Letters*, no. 12, 85).

More, it would seem, was subject to rapid swings between expansive enthusiasm and melancholic skepticism regarding his creation. By the time that the publication was so advanced that it was impossible to draw back, the pendulum of his attitude swung to the opposite extreme of where it had been in late 1516. Just as fervently as he had earlier declared himself to be anxious to see *Utopia* published as quickly as possible, he now pretended that he had not wanted *Utopia* published at all. Writing to William Warham, the archbishop of Canterbury, in January 1517, he declares that *Utopia* was "written in undue haste" and that Peter Giles, allowing his affection to outweigh his judgment, had it printed without his knowledge (*Letters*, no. 13, 89). This is exactly what More had written in his prefatory letter to Giles that was printed in *Utopia*, but it was not what he had told Erasmus, and the inconsistency points yet again to his unresolved ambivalence. He repeats the charge in another letter to a member of the royal court, claiming that Giles had "ravished the first flower" of Utopia's maidenhood without his knowledge (*Letters*, no. 14, 90). His negative mood reaches its blackest depths when he declares to Antonio Bonvisi that *Utopia* is "a book which I think clearly deserves to hide itself away forever in its own island" (*Letters*, no. 15, 90). As much as More felt drawn toward his vision, he also could not bring himself fully to trust it. That was the root cause of his ambivalence.

MORE'S SECOND LETTER TO GILES

After the first edition of *Utopia* appeared More made one final bid to protect himself from being seen as too personally implicated in the work. He did this by strategically placing a second letter to Peter Giles after book 2, so that readers would encounter it immediately after they themselves had tried to interpret the text's meaning. This letter deals with the objections of someone who has criticized *Utopia* on the grounds that, if the story is offered as fact, then it contains some absurdities, and that if it is fiction, then More's own judgment is wanting in some matters (249/1–7). In his reply, More not only defends himself against adverse criticism but also turns the grounds of his defense into a set of guidelines for any future interpretation of his text.

His first tactic is to remind readers that absurdities are bound to exist in any human society, because that is the way life is: "Why should he be so minded as if there were nothing absurd elsewhere in the world or if any of all the philosophers had ever ordered the commonwealth, the ruler, or even the private home without instituting some feature that had better be changed?" (249/31–34). Both human nature and the human situation are imperfect, so that any actual or theoretical attempt to devise a political system is always likely to be imperfect also.

More's second tactic is to claim authorial insight into the absurdities, and by so doing to affirm them as part of his authorial intention. When his critic doubts whether Utopia is real or fictitious, More affirms (with delicious irony) that had he wanted to create a fiction he would have alerted readers to the fact he was doing so: "I should certainly have tempered the fiction so that, if I wanted to abuse the ignorance of common folk, I should have prefixed some indications at least for the more learned to see through our purpose." He would have, he continues, imposed names on the ruler, the river, the city, and the island that "might suggest to the more learned that the island was nowhere, the city a phantom, the river without water, and the ruler without a people." He certainly would not have been "so stupid as to have preferred to use those barbarous and meaningless names, Utopia, Anydrus, Amaurotum, and Ademus" (251/9–21). The irony in all this, of course, is that what he claims he has not done is precisely what he has—and he is reminding readers that these ironic signposts have been placed in the text to alert them to the possibilities of ambiguity and equivocation. Finally, having reminded readers that *Utopia* is a fiction, he proceeds to treat it as if it was not so, by directing the skeptical to seek Hythlodaeus if they doubt his trustworthiness, for he is not yet dead: "I heard lately from travelers coming from Portugal that on last March first he was as hale and spirited as ever. Let them inquire the truth from him or, if they like, dig it out of him with questions" (251/35–253/3). With this final bravura of wit, therefore, More relegates the chance of ever pinning down the truth about *Utopia* to the realms of impossibility, for, paradoxically, Hythlodaeus, though still alive, does not exist.

10

More's Equivocal Masterpiece

More's *Utopia* remains indisputably the most potent work in the genre of writing it initiated. It is archetypally comprehensive because it contains within itself the seeds of its own critique. What More had realized is that all conceptions of the ideal society have to be predicated on a system of order that the basic instincts of human nature are inclined to deny, or at least resist. To provide commodities for all, and to ensure that no one suffers or perpetrates injustice, requires that all members of a society are obliged to work and perform specific duties according to a centrally controlled rational plan. Almost uniquely among utopian writers, More acknowledged in humankind a tendency toward wickedness that was always liable to defeat any utopian efforts to impose such a system of regulation. He also saw the uncanny propensity of the human situation to escape from human attempts to control it. With this realization he created a fiction that allowed the reality of these imperfections to coexist with his blueprint for an ideal state, so that the former could interrogate the viability of the latter, without necessarily destroying the validity of someone entertaining it.

No subsequent utopia has ever achieved this subtle balance between suggesting what is desirable and what is attainable, or what is illusory and what is real. Utopian writers tend to divide into either those who promote their imaginary systems didactically—like Francis Bacon in his *New Atlantis* or Burrhus Frederic Skinner in his *Walden Two*—or those who write dystopias contentiously. Whereas the former exaggerate the benefits to a society of centralized rational planning, the latter seize on the weakness inherent in all utopias: the fact that the need for order can promote tyranny and dehumanization, as the experience in the twentieth century of Stalinist Russia or Maoist China proves. Only More's *Utopia* has the saving grace of being imbued with paradox and ambiguity, which leaves all possibilities open, without definitively denying, or affirming, any of them.

That *Utopia* should have this capacity is a consequence of Thomas More's unique genius. Only very seldom does the world produce a man or woman with his condition of consciousness—the ability to see both the positive and negative aspects of an issue simultaneously without succumbing to neuroticism or, worse, despair.

It is precisely because *Utopia* is the product of such an ambivalent yet comprehensive consciousness and vision that it continues to inspire the human spirit. Its very inconclusiveness has the power to stimulate successive generations of readers into applying their own creative rational energies to solving the problems that More's fantastical *libellus* addresses but does not resolve. In the effects it is capable of working, *Utopia* is truly far greater than the sum of its parts.

Notes

1. Humanism and Reform

1. *The Praise of Folly*, vol. 27 of *The Collected Works of Erasmus*, ed. A. H. T. Levi (Toronto: University of Toronto Press, 1986), 139; hereafter cited as *Erasmus*.

2. See Paul Oskar Kristeller, *Renaissance Thought and Its Sources*, ed. Michael Mooney (New York: Columbia University Press, 1979), 22; Augusto Campana, "The Origin of the Word *Humanist*," *Journal of the Warburg and Courtauld Institutes* 9 (1946): 60–73; and Alistair Fox, "Interpreting English Humanism," in *Reassessing the Henrician Age: Humanism, Politics and Reform, 1500–1550* (Oxford: Basil Blackwell, 1986), 9–33.

3. *John Skelton: The Complete English Poems*, ed. John Scattergood (New Haven, Conn.: Yale University Press, 1983), p. 235, ll. 162–82.

4. See William Roper, *The Lyfe of Sir Thomas Moore, Knighte*, ed. Elsie Vaughan Hitchcock, Early English Text Society, Original Series, no. 197 (London: Oxford University Press, 1935), 9–11; hereafter cited in text.

5. See the discussion by Edward Surtz in CW4, clvi–clxv. See also Elizabeth McCutcheon, "More's *Utopia* and Cicero's *Paradoxa Stoicorum*," in *Thomas More and the Classics*, ed. Ralph Keen and Daniel Kinney (Angers, France: Moreana, 1985), 3–22.

6. For studies concerning the influence of Plato on *Utopia*, see Brendan Bradshaw, "More on Utopia," *Historical Journal* 24 (1981): 1–27; John A. Gueguen, "Reading More's *Utopia* as a Criticism of Plato," in *Quincentennial Essays on St. Thomas More: Selected Papers from the Thomas More College Conference*, ed. Michael J. Moore (Boone, N.C.: Albion, 1978), 43–54; and Judith P. Jones, "The *Philebus* and the Philosophy of Pleasure in Thomas More's *Utopia*," *Moreana*, no. 31–32 (1971): 61–69.

7. For the influence of Lucian on More, see R. Bracht Branham, "Utopian Laughter: Lucian and Thomas More," in *Thomas More and the Classics*, 23–43; Douglas Duncan, *Ben Jonson and the Lucianic Tradition* (Cambridge: Cambridge University Press, 1979); Alistair Fox, *Thomas More: History and Providence* (Oxford: Basil Blackwell, 1982; New Haven, Conn.:

Yale University Press, 1983), 35–44; and Warren W. Wooden, "Thomas More and Lucian: A Study of Satiric Influence and Technique," *University of Mississippi Studies in English* 3 (1972): 43–57.

8. Vespucci's original account is not extant, but a Latin version of it was printed by Waldseemüller in his *Cosmographiae introductio . . . insuper quatuor Americi Vespucij nauigationes* (St. Dié in the Vosges: Walter Ludel, 1507). A modern facsimile reprint and a translation are available in *"Cosmographiae introductio" by Martin Waldseemüller and the English Translation of Joseph Fisher and Franz von Wieser* (Ann Arbor, Mich.: University Microfilms, 1966); hereafter cited as "Vespucci."

2. The Importance of the Work

1. A phrase taken from the letter to Thomas Lupset by Guillaume Budé, a French humanist contemporary of More's, printed in the 1518 edition of *Utopia* (15/22–23).

2. See Silvio Zavala, "Sir Thomas More in New Spain," in *Essential Articles for the Study of Thomas More*, ed. R. S. Sylvester and G. P. Marc'hadour (Hamden, Conn.: Archon Books, 1977).

3. R. W. Chambers, *Thomas More* (London: Jonathan Cape, 1935), 125; hereafter cited in text.

4. For a comprehensive list of utopias and dystopias written between 1500 and 1750, see *St. Thomas More: A Preliminary Bibliography of His Works and of Moreana to the Year 1750*, comp. R. W. Gibson and J. Max Patrick (New Haven, Conn., and London: Yale University Press, 1961), 291–412; hereafter cited in text. See also the survey by Frank E. Manuel and Fritzie P. Manuel, *Utopian Thought in the Western World* (Oxford: Basil Blackwell, 1979).

5. See Niccolò Macchiavelli, *The Prince*, trans. with an introduction by George Bull (Harmondsworth, England: Penguin, 1961), 91.

3. Critical Reception

1. See also P. Albert Duhamel, "Medievalism of More's *Utopia*," in *Essential Articles*, 234–50.

2. J. H. Hexter, "A Window to the Future: The Radicalism of *Utopia*," Introduction, pt. 1, *CW*4, cv–cxxiv. See also Hexter's *More's Utopia: The Biography of an Idea* (1952; rpt., New York: Harper Torchbooks, 1965); Frederic Seebohm, *The Oxford Reformers*, 3d ed. (London: Longmans, 1911); and Hubertus Schulte Herbrüggen, "More's *Utopia* as a Paradigm," in *Essential Articles*, 251–62. Seebohm's volume is hereafter cited in text.

3. See, respectively, Bradshaw, "More on Utopia"; Thomas I. White, "Aristotle and *Utopia*," *Renaissance Quarterly* 29 (1976): 635–75; and Martin N. Raitiere, "More's *Utopia* and *The City of God*," *Studies in the Renaissance* 20 (1973): 144–68.

4. For this view, see especially C. S. Lewis, *English Literature in the Six-teenth Century Excluding Drama* (Oxford: Clarendon Press, 1954); hereafter cited in text. The relevant discussion is reprinted in *Essential Articles*, 388–401.

5. See *CW*4, 43/5–16; cf. William Roper and Nicholas Harpsfield, *Lives of Saint Thomas More*, ed. E. E. Reynolds (London: Dent, 1963), 110; here-after cited in text.

6. William Tyndale, *The Practice of Prelates*, vol. 1 of *The Works of the English Reformers: William Tyndale, Robert Barnes, and John Frith* (London: E. Palmer, 1831), 448.

7. Vol. 4 of *The Acts and Monuments of John Foxe, With a Preliminary Dissertation by the Rev. George Townsend, M. A.*, ed. S. R. Cattley (London: R. B. Seeley and W. Burnside, 1841), 643.

8. Vol. 8 of *CW, The Confutation of Tyndale's Answer*, ed. Louis A. Schuster and others (1973), pt. 1, 178; hereafter cited as *CW*8.

9. See James K. McConica, "The Recusant Reputation of Thomas More," in *Essential Articles*, 136–49.

10. Karl Kautsky, *Thomas More and His Utopia*, trans. H. J. Stenning (London: A. & C. Black, 1927), 160.

11. Russell Ames, *Citizen Thomas More and His Utopia* (Princeton, N.J.: Princeton University Press, 1949), 6.

12. This type of approach was inaugurated by Dermot Fenlon, "England and Europe: *Utopia* and Its Aftermath," *Transactions of the Royal Historical Society* 25 (1975): 115–35.

13. Quentin Skinner, "Sir Thomas More's *Utopia* and the Language of Renaissance Humanism," in *Ideas in Context: The Languages of Political Theory in Early-Modern Europe*, ed. Anthony Pagden (Cambridge: Cambridge University Press, 1987), 123–57, which substantially modifies the same author's view of *Utopia* as stated in his earlier book, *The Foundations of Modern Political Thought*, vol. 1 (Cambridge: Cambridge University Press, 1978).

14. George M. Logan, *The Meaning of More's Utopia* (Princeton, N.J.: Princeton University Press, 1983), 268.

15. Gilbert Burnet, *The History of the Reformation of the Church of England. The Third Part, Being a Supplement to the Two Volumes Formerly Published* (London: J. Churchill, 1715), pt. 3, bk. 1, p. 31.

16. James Mackintosh, *The Life of Sir Thomas More* (London: Long-mans, 1844), and T. E. Bridgett, *Life and Writings of Sir Thomas More* (London: Burns and Oates, 1891).

17. Edward L. Surtz, *The Praise of Wisdom: A Commentary on the Reli-gious and Moral Problems and Backgrounds of St. Thomas More's Utopia* (Chicago: Loyola University Press, 1957), 1–20.

18. See, for example, W. J. Barnes, "Irony and the English Apprehension of Renewal," *Queen's Quarterly* 73 (1966): 357–76, and Harry Berger, Jr., "The Renaissance Imagination: Second World and Green World," *Centennial Review* 9 (1965): 36–77.

19. T. S. Dorsch, "Sir Thomas More and Lucian: An Interpretation of *Utopia*," *Archiv für das Studium der neueren Sprachen und Literaturen* 203 (1967): 349–63.

20. See, in particular, David M. Bevington, "The Dialogue in *Utopia*: Two Sides to the Question," *Studies in Philology* 58 (1961): 496–509, and Robbin S. Johnson, *More's Utopia: Ideal and Illusion* (New Haven, Conn.: Yale University Press, 1969).

21. Joel B. Altman, *The Tudor Play of Mind: Rhetorical Inquiry and the Development of Elizabethan Drama* (Berkeley: University of California Press, 1978), 80.

22. R. S. Sylvester, "*Si Hythlodaeo credimus*: Vision and Revision in Thomas More's *Utopia*," *Soundings* 51 (1968): 272–89.

23. Elizabeth McCutcheon, *My Dear Peter: The Ars Poetica and Hermeneutics for More's Utopia* (Angers, France: Moreanum, 1983), 9.

24. Stephen Greenblatt, *Renaissance Self-fashioning from More to Shakespeare* (Chicago and London: University of Chicago Press, 1980), 13.

4. Approaching Utopia

1. Desiderius Erasmus, "Letter to Ulrich von Hutten," in *Erasmus*, 7, no. 999, 24/282–83.

2. See the hypothetical reconstruction by J. H. Hexter in *CW*4, xv–xxiii.

3. *St. Thomas More: Selected Letters*, ed. Elizabeth Frances Rogers (New Haven, Conn., and London: Yale University Press, 1961), no. 6, 73; hereafter cited as *Letters*.

4. See the letter of Giles to Busleyden, *CW*4, 23/21–26.

5. The Eutopia within Book 2

1. See More, *Utopia*, ed. George M. Logan and Robert M. Adams (Cambridge: Cambridge University Press, 1989), 42; hereafter cited as "*Utopia*, ed. Logan and Adams."

2. See Elizabeth McCutcheon's excellent and indispensible article "Denying the Contrary: More's Use of Litotes in *Utopia*," in *Essential Articles*, 263–74.

3. See Franklin B. Williams, "Utopia's Chicken's Come Home to Roost," *Moreana* 18, no. 69 (March 1981): 77–78.

4. See Arthur Barker, "*Clavis Moreana*: The Yale Edition of Thomas More," in *Essential Articles*, 215–28, esp. 219–23.

6. Irony and Satire in Book 2

1. I am indebted to the suggestions of Logan and Adams (*Utopia*, xxiv) for this line of thought.

2. Aristotle, *The Politics*, ed. Stephen Everson (Cambridge: Cambridge University Press, 1988), bk. 7, p. 156; hereafter cited as *Politics*.

3. For an excellent discussion of this type of paradox in *Utopia*, see Arthur F. Kinney, "Rhetoric as Poetic: Humanist Fiction in the Renaissance," *ELH* 43 (1976): 413–43, and Kinney's *Rhetoric and Poetic in Thomas More's Utopia*, Humana Civilitas, vol. 5 (Malibu: Undena Publications, 1979).

4. See Alistair Fox, "Chaucer, More, and English Humanism," in *Rulers, Religion and Rhetoric in Early Modern England: A Festschrift for Geoffrey Elton from His Australasian Friends, Parergon*, n.s. 6 (1988): 63–75, esp. 67.

7. Religious Faith in Utopia

1. See More, "Verses for the Book of Fortune," in *The Workes of Sir Thomas More Knyght, Sometyme Lorde Chauncellor of England, Wrytten by Him in the Englysh Tonge*, ed. William Rastell (London: W. Rastell, 1557), sig. Cviii^V. For commentary on these earlier works, see Fox, *Thomas More: History and Providence*, 11–23.

2. See St. Augustine, *The City of God (De civitate Dei)*, vol. 1, trans. John Healey, ed. R. V. G. Tasker with an introduction by Sir Ernest Barker (London: Dent, 1945), 1–2.

3. I have here chosen the translation offered by Logan and Adams in preference to that given in the Yale edition. The Latin text reads: " . . . uelut in unum finem diuersa uia commigrant" (*CW4*, 232/6–7).

4. Vol. 6 of *CW. A Dialogue Concerning Heresies*, ed. Thomas M. C. Lawler, Germain Marc'hadour, and Richard C. Marius (1981), 146/33–34; hereafter cited as *CW6*. *CW8*, pt. 1, 248/12–249/16.

5. I have modified the translation given in the Yale edition by substituting "wiser" for Yale's "saner" as the word for More's "*prudentiores*."

8. The Context and Argument of Book 1

1. William Shakespeare, *A Midsummer Night's Dream*, ed. Wolfgang Clemen (New York: Signet, 1963), 5.1.14–17.

2. William Shakespeare, *Hamlet*, ed. Edward Hubler (New York: Signet, 1963), 3.2.217–19.

3. See Geoffrey Elton, "Thomas More, Councillor," in *St. Thomas More: Action and Contemplation*, ed. R. S. Sylvester (New Haven, Conn.: Yale University Press, 1972), 90. An argument has been made for an earlier date (i.e., late 1516), but the evidence remains circumstantial and still puts the date of More's entry at a considerable time after he first received the king's offer. See Jerry Mermel, "Preparations for a Oolitic Life: Sir Thomas More's

Entry into the King's Service," *Journal of Medieval and Renaissance Studies* 7 (1977): 53–66.

4. Vol. 3 of *CW*, pt. 2, *Latin Poems*, ed. Clarence Miller and others (1984), 229–31, no. 198 (my italics); hereafter cited as *CW3*.

5. Cicero, *De officiis*, trans. Walter Miller (London: Heinemann; Cambridge, Mass.: Harvard University Press, 1968), 1.21.71; hereafter cited as *De officiis*.

9. The Inconclusiveness of Utopia

1. For a vigorous debate on whether "More's" concluding remarks in Utopia are serious or ironic, see J. H. Hexter, "Intention, Words, and Meaning: The Case of More's *Utopia*," *New Literary History* 6 (1975): 529–41, and Ward Allen, "The Tone of More's Farewell to *Utopia*: A Reply to J. H. Hexter," *Moreana*, no. 51 (1976): 108–18.

2. Vol. 5 of *CW*, *Responsio ad Lutherum*, ed. John M. Headley (1969), 275/31–35.

3. Vol. 12 of *CW*, *A Dialogue of Comfort Against Tribulation*, ed. Louis L. Martz and Frank Manley (1976), 179/18–180/28.

Bibliography

PRIMARY WORKS

Collected Works

The Workes of Sir Thomas More Knyght, Sometyme Lorde Chauncellor of England, Wrytten by Him in the Englysh Tonge. Edited by William Rastell. London: W. Rastell, 1557. Available in a facsimile reprint, with an introduction by K. J. Wilson, by Scolar Press, London, 1978. Contains material not yet published in the Yale edition.

The Yale Edition of the Complete Works of St. Thomas More. Various editors. 14 vols. New Haven, Conn., and London: Yale University Press 1963–. The definitive edition.

Letters

The Correspondence of Sir Thomas More. Edited by Elizabeth Frances Rogers. Princeton, N.J.: Princeton University Press, 1947. Remains the standard edition.

St. Thomas More: Selected Letters. Edited by Elizabeth Frances Rogers. New Haven, Conn., and London: Yale University Press, 1961. Contains English translations of More's most important letters written in Latin.

Editions of Utopia

The Yale Edition of the Complete Works of St. Thomas More. Vol. 4, *Utopia,* edited by J. H. Hexter and Edward Surtz. New Haven, Conn., and London: Yale University Press, 1965. The standard edition, containing the Latin text and a facing translation by C. G. Richards, extended introductory essays by Hexter and Surtz, and a very full commentary by Surtz. The translation at key points has, however, been severely criticized.

Utopia. In *The Essential Thomas More,* edited by James J. Greene and John P. Dolan. New York and Toronto: New American Library, 1967. This anthology contains a good translation of *Utopia* by John P. Dolan, but it lacks the parerga.

Utopia: A New Translation, Backgrounds, Criticism. Translated and edited by Robert M. Adams. New York and London: W. W. Norton, 1975. A useful student text on account of its excellent translation and generous selection of critical extracts, but lacks some of the parerga.

More's "Utopia" and Its Critics. Edited by Ligeia Gallagher. Chicago: Scott, Foresman & Co., 1964. Contains a useful selection of critical extracts.

Utopia. Edited by George M. Logan and Robert M. Adams. Cambridge: Cambridge University Press, 1989. The best edition for the use of students and the general reader. Contains most of the parerga.

Utopia: The "Utopia" of Sir Thomas More. Edited by J. H. Lupton. Oxford: Clarendon Press, 1895. Contains an unmodernized version of the Tudor translation by Ralph Robinson.

More's "Utopia" and "A Dialogue of Comfort." Introduced by John Warrington. London: Dent; New York: Dutton, 1910; reprinted 1965. Contains a modernized version of the Tudor translation by Ralph Robinson.

Utopia. Translated and edited by Paul Turner. Harmondsworth, England: Penguin, 1965. A racy translation that emphasizes the Lucianic elements, but Turner really distorts by depriving the names of their inherent ambiguity.

SECONDARY WORKS

Books

Adams, Robert P. *The Better Part of Valor: More, Erasmus, Colet, and Vives, on Humanism, War, and Peace, 1496–1535.* Seattle: University of Washington Press, 1962. Sees *Utopia* as a humanist vision of a radically improved social order based on the elimination of war as a man-made evil.

Altman, Joel B. *The Tudor Play of Mind: Rhetorical Inquiry and the Development of Elizabethan Drama.* Berkeley: University of California Press, 1978. Emphasizes the influence of the rhetorical tradition on the literary form of *Utopia.*

Ames, Russell. *Citizen Thomas More and His Utopia.* Princeton, N.J.: Princeton University Press, 1949. Interprets *Utopia* as a manifestation of capitalism's attack on feudalism, arguing that the book is fundamentally republican and bourgeois in its values.

Baker-Smith, Dominic. *More's Utopia.* London and New York: HarperCollinsAcademic, 1991. Explores *Utopia* as a reflection on political idealism, particularly in relation to More's classical and Christian sources.

Bolchazy, L., ed. *A Concordance to the Utopia of St. Thomas More and a Frequency Word List.* Hildesheim and New York: Georg Olms Verlag, 1978. An invaluable concordance to the Latin text of *Utopia.*

Bridgett, T. E. *Life and Writings of Sir Thomas More.* London: Burns & Oates, 1891. The traditional Catholic view of More, regarding Hythlodaeus as More's mouthpiece in book 1 but divorcing him from the author concerning aspects of book 2.

Burnet, Gilbert. *The History of the Reformation of the Church of England. The Third Part, Being a Supplement to the Two Volumes Formerly Published.* London: J. Churchill, 1715.

Campbell, W. E. *More's Utopia and His Social Teaching.* London: Eyre & Spottiswoode, 1930. A Roman Catholic interpretation that assumes that More's view of social truth depended on his supernatural faith.

Chambers, R. W. *Thomas More.* London: Jonathan Cape, 1935. Still the best biography of More, although it should be supplemented by the revisionist studies of John A. Guy and Richard Marius, and by Geoffrey Elton's important essay.

Davis, J. C. *Utopia and the Ideal Society.* Cambridge: Cambridge University Press, 1981. Examines *Utopia* in the context of other sixteenth- and seventeenth-century utopian writings.

Donner, H. W. *Introduction to Utopia.* London: Sidgwick & Jackson, 1945. Follows Chambers in viewing *Utopia* as a moral fable that invites readers not to copy it but to surpass it.

Duncan, Douglas. *Ben Jonson and the Lucianic Tradition.* Cambridge: Cambridge University Press, 1979. Contains a discussion of the ludic method of *Utopia.*

Fleisher, Martin. *Radical Reform and Political Persuasion in the Life and Writings of Thomas More.* Travaux d'humanisme et Renaissance, 132. Geneva: Librairie Droz, 1973. Sees *Utopia* as designed to actualize reformist aspirations by the use of life-giving or inspiring means, so that the substance of reform is inseparable from the method of reform.

Fox, Alistair. *Politics and Literature in the Reigns of Henry VII and Henry VIII.* Oxford: Basil Blackwell, 1989. Chapter 6 examines the paradoxicality of *Utopia.*

_____. *Thomas More: History and Providence.* Oxford: Basil Blackwell, 1982. Places *Utopia* in the context of More's intellectual career.

Fox, Alistair, and John Guy. *Reassessing the Henrician Age: Humanism, Politics and Reform, 1500–1550.* Oxford: Basil Blackwell, 1986. Contains a brief consideration of *Utopia* in the context of English humanism.

Greenblatt, Stephen. *Renaissance Self-fashioning from More to Shakespeare.* Chicago and London: University of Chicago Press, 1980. Applies a neo-historicism approach to *Utopia,* interpreting it in terms of postmodern theories of authorial identity formation.

Bibliography

Guy, John A. *The Public Career of Sir Thomas More*. Brighton, England: Harvester, 1980. Contains essential information on the context surrounding *Utopia*.

Hexter, J. H. *More's Utopia: The Biography of an Idea*. 1952; reprint, New York: Harper Torchbooks, 1965. A seminal study that demonstrates that book 1 was composed after book 2; treats *Utopia* as a serious work of reform.

Johnson, Robbin S. *More's Utopia: Ideal and Illusion*. New Haven, Conn.: Yale University Press, 1969. Argues that *Utopia* is less a final goal and more an attitude or stance.

Jones, Judith P. *Thomas More*. Boston: Twayne Publishers, 1979. A useful survey of More's life and works, containing an annotated bibliography.

Kautsky, Karl. *Thomas More and His Utopia*, translated by H. J. Stenning. London: A. & C. Black, 1927. The most famous Marxist analysis of *Utopia*.

Kinney, Arthur F. *Rhetoric and Poetic in Thomas More's Utopia*. Humana Civilitas. Vol. 5. Malibu: Undena Publications, 1979. Expands on the insights of his 1976 article in *ELH*.

Lewis, C. S. *English Literature in the Sixteenth Century Excluding Drama*. Oxford: Clarendon Press, 1954. Advances the view that *Utopia* is a jeu d'esprit.

Logan, George M. *The Meaning of More's "Utopia."* Princeton, N.J.: Princeton University Press, 1983. An important consideration of the intellectual sources and analogues of *Utopia*.

McCutcheon, Elizabeth. *My Dear Peter: The Ars Poetica and Hermeneutics for More's Utopia*. Angers, France: Moreanum, 1983. An indispensable work on the nature and function of More's preface to *Utopia*.

Mackintosh, James. *The Life of Sir Thomas More*. London: Longmans, 1844. Considers that More regarded various aspects of *Utopia* "with almost every possible degree of approbation and shade of assent."

Manuel, Frank E., and Fritzie P. Manuel. *Utopian Thought in the Western World*. Oxford: Basil Blackwell, 1979. A magisterial survey of utopian writing, including an excellent discussion of *Utopia*.

Marin, Louis. *Utopics: The Semiological Play of Textual Spaces*. Atlantic Highlands, N.J.: Humanities Press International, 1984; reprint, 1990. A semiotic approach that studies More's *Utopia* as the basis for a theoretical reflection of utopic signifying practices.

Marius, Richard. *Thomas More*. London and Melbourne: J. M. Dent, 1984. A revisionist biography that takes issue with many of the assumptions of R. W. Chambers and Roman Catholic biographers.

Mason, H. A. *Humanism and Poetry in the Early Tudor Period: An Essay*. London: Jonathan Cape, 1959. Examines *Utopia* as a creative response to the classics in the light of the contradictions in More's personality.

117

Moore, Michael J., ed. *Quincentennial Essays on St. Thomas More: Selected Papers from the Thomas More College Conference.* Boone, N.C.: Albion, 1978. Contains many valuable essays on *Utopia.*

Murphy, Clare M., Henri Gibaud, and Mario A. Di Cesare, eds. *Miscellanea Moreana: Essays for Germain Marc'hadour.* Binghamton, N.Y.: Medieval and Renaissance Texts and Studies, 1989. Contains a number of essays and notes on *Utopia.*

Nelson, William, ed. *Twentieth Century Interpretations of Utopia: A Collection of Critical Essays.* Englewood Cliffs, N.J.: Prentice-Hall, 1968. A useful collection of important critical essays but now rather dated.

Norbrook, David. *Politics and Poetry in the English Renaissance.* London: Routledge & Kegan Paul, 1984. A neo-Marxist approach emphasizing the split between the ideas embodied in *Utopia* and the realities of Henry VIII's court.

Seebohm, Frederic. *The Oxford Reformers.* 3d ed. London: Longmans, 1911. Articulates the "Protestant" view of *Utopia* by assuming that its point consists in the contrast presented by its ideal commonwealth to the condition and habits of the European commonwealths of the period.

Skinner, Quentin. *The Foundations of Modern Political Thought.* 2 vols. Cambridge: Cambridge University Press, 1978. Develops the idea that *Utopia* offers a critique of humanism.

Sullivan, E. D. S., ed. *The Utopian Vision: Seven Essays on the Quincentennial of Sir Thomas More.* San Diego: San Diego State University Press, 1983. A stimulating collection of essays on aspects of utopian writing and the utopian genre generally.

Surtz, Edward L. *The Praise of Pleasure: Philosophy, Education, and Communism in More's Utopia.* Cambridge, Mass.: Harvard University Press, 1957. This, together with the following entry, presents the traditional Roman Catholic view of *Utopia.*

_____. *The Praise of Wisdom: A Commentary on the Religious and Moral Problems and Backgrounds of St. Thomas More's Utopia.* Chicago: Loyola University Press, 1957.

Sylvester, R. S., ed. *St. Thomas More: Action and Contemplation.* New Haven, Conn.: Yale University Press, 1972. Contains Geoffrey Elton's important essay on More's entry into the royal service.

Sylvester, R. S., and G. P. Marc'hadour, eds. *Essential Articles for the Study of Thomas More.* Hamden, Conn.: Archon Books, 1977. An indispensable collection of articles on *Utopia* and on all aspects of More's life and works.

Wilson, K. J. *Incomplete Fictions: The Formation of English Renaissance Dialogue.* Washington, D.C.: Catholic University of America Press, 1985. Argues that More transforms the dialogue genre through his invention of dramatic characters.

Bibliography

Articles

Allen, Peter R. "Utopia and European Humanism: The Function of the Prefatory Letters and Verses." *Studies in the Renaissance* 10 (1963): 91–107. Argues that the parerga are deliberately designed to control the reader's interpretation of *Utopia*.

Allen, Ward. "The Tone of More's Farewell to *Utopia*: A Reply to J. H. Hexter." *Moreana*, no. 51 (1976): 108–18. Argues against J. H. Hexter's view that "More's" final argument in *Utopia* is "palpably silly and insincere," proposing instead that More wishes to encourage an ambivalent and puzzled view in the reader.

Barker, Arthur. "*Clavis Moreana*: The Yale Edition of Thomas More." *Journal of English and Germanic Philology* 65 (1966): 318–30. Reprinted in Sylvester and Marc'hadour, eds., *Essential Articles*, 215–28. Speculates on the significance of the name changes in *Utopia*.

Barnes, W. J. "Irony and the English Apprehension of Renewal." *Queen's Quarterly* 73 (1966): 357–76. Shows how the addition of book 1 transforms book 2 from a straightforward narrative into an ironic representation.

Berger, Harry, Jr. "The Renaissance Imagination: Second World and Green World." *Centennial Review* 9 (1965): 36–77. Argues that Hythlodaeus is depicted ironically, and that the self-enclosed spatiality of Hythlodaeus's green world is a womblike retreat protected from the outside world. Reprinted in Robert M. Adams, ed., *Utopia: A New Translation, Backgrounds, Criticism*, 203–12.

Bevington, David M. "The Dialogue in *Utopia*: Two Sides to the Question." *Studies in Philology* 58 (1961): 496–509. Sees in *Utopia* the impartial presentation of two points of view representing the polarities of More's mind.

Bradshaw, Brendan. "More on Utopia." *Historical Journal* 24 (1981): 1–27. Attacks J. H. Hexter's analysis of *Utopia* as a seriously presented ideal society, and reasserts the traditional Roman Catholic view as formulated by Edward L. Surtz.

Branham, R. Bracht. "Utopian Laughter: Lucian and Thomas More." In *Thomas More and the Classics*, ed. Ralph Keen and Daniel Kinney, 23–43. Angers, France: Moreana, 1985. Argues that More transforms his Lucianic starting points by purging qualities that were unsuited to his own very different purposes.

Coogan, Augusto. "*Nunc vivo ut volo*." *Moreana*, no. 31-32 (1971): 29–45. Surveys the scholarship on Hythlodaeus.

Dorsch, T. S. "Sir Thomas More and Lucian: An Interpretation of *Utopia*." *Archiv für das studium der neueren sprachen und literaturen* 203 (1967): 349–63. Argues that More turns *Utopia* into a dystopia through the use of Lucianic irony.

119

Duhamel, P. Albert. "Medievalism of More's Utopia." *Studies in Philology* 52 (1955): 99–126. Reprinted in Sylvester and Marc'hadour, eds., *Essential Articles*, 234–50. Argues that the implicit heuristic method that determined the content of *Utopia* is medieval.

Elliott, Robert C. "The Shape of Utopia." *ELH* 30 (1963): 317–34. A critique of the Roman Catholic interpretation of *Utopia*, especially as presented by Edward L. Surtz, which looks at the work as satire. Reprinted in Robert M. Adams, ed., *Utopia: A New Translation, Backgrounds, Criticism,* 177–92.

Elton, Geoffrey. "Thomas More, Councillor (1517–1529)." In *St. Thomas More: Action and Contemplation*, edited by R. S. Sylvester. New Haven, Conn.: Yale University Press, 1972. Dismisses the idea that More was reluctant to join the court.

Fenlon, Dermot. "England and Europe: Utopia and Its Aftermath." *Transactions of the Royal Historical Society* 25 (1975): 115–35. Sees *Utopia* as offering a critique of the humanists' reform strategy as being based on an illusion.

Fox, Alistair. "Chaucer, More, and English Humanism." In *Rulers, Religion, and Rhetoric in Early Modern England: A Festschrift for Geoffrey Elton from His Australasian Friends. Parergon,* n.s. 6 (1988): 63–75.

Gordon, Walter M. "The Monastic Achievement and More's Utopian Dream." *Medievalia et Humanistica,* n.s. 9 (1979): 199–214.

Grace, Damian. "*Utopia*: A Dialectical Interpretation." In *Miscellanea Moreana: Essays for Germain Marc'hadour,* edited by Clare M. Murphy, Henri Gibaud, and Mario A. Di Cesare, 273–302. Binghamton, N.Y.: Medieval and Renaissance Texts and Studies, 1989. The tactical ambiguities and paradoxes of *Utopia* are designed to make it dialectical, bringing into relationship at least two sets of intentions but leaving unresolved the issues they address.

Greene, James J. "*Utopia* and Early More Biography." *Moreana,* no. 31–32 (1971): 199–207. Suggests causes for the hostility of Roman Catholic orthodoxy toward *Utopia* by tracing the reactions to it of More's early biographers.

Gueguen, John A. "Reading More's *Utopia* as a Criticism of Plato." In *Quincentennial Essays on St. Thomas More: Selected Papers from the Thomas More College Conference,* edited by Michael J. Moore, 43–54. Boone, N.C.: Albion, 1978. Views More as a consistent contributor to the cultural, and especially the spiritual, heritage of medieval Christendom, who pursued a fundamental reformation of Platonic theology.

Heisermann, A. R. "Satire in the *Utopia.*" *PMLA* 78 (1963): 163–74. Places *Utopia* in the tradition of satiric works that teach virtue by attacking vice.

Herbrüggen, Hubertus Schulte. "More's *Utopia* as a Paradigm." In Sylvester and Marc'hadour, eds., *Essential Articles*, 251–62. Argues that the work's structure centers on the idea of Utopian ideality founded in the ethics of its citizens.

Hexter, J. H. "Intention, Words, and Meaning: The Case of More's *Utopia.*" *New Literary History* 6 (1975): 529–41. Attacks the view that "More's" reaction to Hythlodaeus's account at the conclusion of *Utopia* is to be taken seriously.

Jones, Judith P. "The Philebus and the Philosophy of Pleasure in Thomas More's *Utopia.*" *Moreana*, no. 31–32 (1971): 61–69. Views the hedonism of *Utopia* as another manifestation of the pervasive Platonic influence on the book, especially that of Plato's *Philebus.*

Khanna, Lee Cullen. "Utopia: The Case for Open-mindedness in the Commonwealth." *Moreana*, no. 31–32 (1971): 91–105. Argues that the two books of *Utopia* form a self-contained literary unit whose consistent theme is the importance of open-mindedness for the improvement of the social order.

Kinney, Arthur F. "Rhetoric as Poetic: Humanist Fiction in the Renaissance." *ELH* 43 (1976): 413–43. Argues that *Utopia* is a *declamatio* that is also a mock-encomium and hence one that leads to an inherent disputation. Sees *Utopia* as a compliment and complement to Erasmus's *Praise of Folly.*

McConica, James K. "The Recusant Reputation of Thomas More." In Sylvester and Marc'hadour, eds., *Essential Articles*, 136–49. Identifies the unease shown toward *Utopia* by More's Roman Catholic descendants and admirers.

McCutcheon, Elizabeth. "Denying the Contrary: More's Use of Litotes in *Utopia.*" *Moreana*, no. 31–32 (1971): 107–21. Reprinted in Sylvester and Marc'hadour, eds, *Essential Articles*, 263–74. A very important article that demonstrates how the use of litotes manifests the paradoxical double vision of *Utopia.*

_____. "More's *Utopia* and Cicero's *Paradoxa Stoicorum.*" In *Thomas More and the Classics*, edited by Ralph Keen and Daniel Kinney, 3–22. Angers, France: Moreana, 1985. Argues that Cicero's work illuminates More's habits of thought, his artistry, and his values, but that More goes far beyond Cicero in his development of paradox.

McKinnon, Dana G. "The Marginal Glosses in More's *Utopia*: The Character of the Commentator." In *Renaissance Papers*, edited by Dennis G. Donovan, 11–19. Durham, N.C.: Southeastern Renaissance Conference, 1971.

Mermel, Jerry. "Preparations for a Politic Life: Sir Thomas More's Entry into the King's Service." *Journal of Medieval and Renaissance Studies* 7

(1977): 53–66. Argues that More's entry into the royal service was earlier than usually supposed, and that Erasmus knew of it.

Nagel, Alan F. "Lies and the Limitable Inane: Contradiction in More's *Utopia.*" *Renaissance Quarterly* 26 (1973): 173–80. Explores the etymological play present in the names in *Utopia* as More's means of internally defining the limits of the fiction.

Olin, John C. "Erasmus' *Adagia* and More's *Utopia.*" In *Miscellanea Moreana: Essays for Germain Marc'hadour*, edited by Clare M. Murphy, Henri Gibaud, and Mario A. Di Cesare, 127–36. Binghamton, N.Y.: Medieval and Renaissance Texts and Studies, 1989. Examines the correspondence between *Utopia* and the Erasmian adage "Friends Have All Things in Common."

Raitiere, Martin N. "More's *Utopia* and *The City of God.*" *Studies in the Renaissance* 20 (1973): 144–68. Argues that More's Augustinian attitude continually qualifies the validity of his humanistic assumptions.

Rudat, Wolfgang E. H. "More's Raphael Hythloday: Missing the Point in *Utopia* Once More?" *Moreana*, no. 69 (1981): 41–64. Argues that More sets traps for the reader, yet at the same time builds in devices that might warn the more perceptive reader.

Schaeffer, John D. "Socratic Method in More's *Utopia.*" *Moreana*, no. 69 (1981): 5–20. Regards the irony of the work as focusing on the paradoxes involved in changing individuals and society for the better, and as playing on the relationship of rhetoric and dialogue, Cicero and Socrates, and Hythlodaeus and "More."

Schoeck, R. J. "'A Nursery of Correct and Useful Institutions'": On Reading More's *Utopia* as Dialogue." *Moreana*, no. 22 (1969): 19–32. Reprinted in Sylvester and Marc'hadour, eds., *Essential Articles*, 281–89. Regards *Utopia* as having a serious purpose but one argued through an ironic structure, and as inviting a response that is both engaged and detached.

_____. "More, Plutarch, and King Agis: Spartan History and the Meaning of *Utopia.*" *Philological Quarterly* 35 (1956): 366–75. Reprinted in Sylvester and Marc'hadour, eds., *Essential Articles*, 275–80. Proposes a parallel between *Utopia* and the story of King Agis IV of Sparta as told in Plutarch's *Lives.*

_____. "The Ironic and the Prophetic: Towards Reading More's *Utopia* as a Multidisciplinary Work." In *Quincentennial Essays on St. Thomas More: Selected Papers from the Thomas More College Conference*, edited by Michael J. Moore, 124–34. Boone, N.C.: Albion, 1978. Suggests that *Utopia* cannot be read only as a literary, political, educational, polemical treatise, or as a jeu d'esprit, but must be read holistically as a multidisciplinary work.

Bibliography

Skinner, Quentin. "More's Utopia." *Past and Present* 38 (1967): 153–68. An important critique of the Yale edition.

―――. "Sir Thomas More's Utopia and the Language of Renaissance Humanism." In *Ideas in Context: The Languages of Political Theory in Early-Modern Europe*, edited by Anthony Pagden, 123–57. Cambridge: Cambridge University Press, 1987. Argues that Hythlodaeus's Platonic commitment to the contemplative life (*otium*) is brought into conflict with a Ciceronian defence of the active life (*negotium*).

Sylvester, R. S. "'Si Hythlodaeo credimus': Vision and Revision in Thomas More's *Utopia*." *Soundings* 51 (1968): 272–89. Reprinted in Sylvester and Marc'hadour, eds., *Essential Articles*, 290–301. An important consideration of the parerga to *Utopia* and of the ways in which More sustains the ambiguity of the work.

Volgin, Vyacheslav. "Sir Thomas More." *Review of World Events* 39 (15 February 1953): 14–15. Reprinted in *More's Utopia and Its Critics*, edited by Ligeia Gallagher, 106–8. Chicago: Scott, Foresman & Co., 1964. Sees *Utopia* as an unequivocal blueprint for communism.

Weiner, Andrew D. "Raphael's Eutopia and More's Utopia: Christian Humanism and the Limits of Reason." *Huntington Library Quarterly* 39 (1975): 1–27. Argues that *Utopia* is neither a satire nor a philosophical discourse but a rhetorical persuasion that uses reason as a means of attacking abuse while showing the inadequacy of reason to correct those abuses.

White, Thomas I. "Aristotle and *Utopia*." *Renaissance Quarterly* 29 (1976): 635–75. Proposes that More's knowledge of Aristotle and the influence of Aristotle on *Utopia* have been slighted.

―――. "*Festivitas, Utilitas, et Opes*: The Concluding Irony and Philosophical Purpose of Thomas More's *Utopia*." In *Quincentennial Essays on St. Thomas More: Selected Papers from the Thomas More College Conference*, edited by Michael J. Moore, 134–50. Boone, N.C.: Albion, 1978. Argues for an ironic reading, based on the assumption that More's attitudes at the point in his career when *Utopia* was written made it impossible for him to intend seriously the criticisms leveled by "More" at the end of the work.

Williams, Franklin B. "Utopia's Chickens Come Home to Roost." *Moreana*, no. 69 (March 1981): 77–78.

Wooden, Warren W. "Anti-Scholastic Satire in Sir Thomas More's *Utopia*." *Sixteenth Century Journal* 8, no. 2 (1977): 29–45. Sees Hythlodaeus as the focus of a pervasive secondary attack in *Utopia*, at the level of intellectual satire, on the scholastic theologians and Schoolmen.

―――. "A Reconsideration of the Parerga of Thomas More's *Utopia*." In *Quincentennial Essays on St. Thomas More: Selected Papers from the Thomas More College Conference*, edited by Michael J. Moore, 151–60.

Boone, N.C.: Albion, 1978. Sees the parerga as preparing the reader for a work more serious than the classical Lucianic prototype suggests, yet featuring a broad and pervasive vein of humor and satire.

_____. "Thomas More and Lucian: A Study of Satiric Influence and Technique." *University of Mississippi Studies in English* 13 (1972): 43–57. Traces More's debt to the tradition of Lucianic satire, focusing on the characterization of Hythlodaeus as the *philosophus gloriosus*.

Bibliographies

Geritz, Albert J. "Recent Studies in More (1977–1990)." *English Literary Renaissance* 22 (1991): 112–40. Contains a comprehensive annotated list of studies of *Utopia* between 1977 and 1990 that complements the earlier survey by Judith Jones.

Gibson, R. W., and J. Max Patrick. *St. Thomas More: A Preliminary Bibliography of His Works and of Moreana to the Year 1750.* New Haven, Conn., and London: Yale University Press, 1961. Contains a comprehensive bibliography of utopias and dystopias, as well as full bibliographical details concerning editions of More's works.

Jones, Judith Paterson. "Recent Studies in More." *English Literary Renaissance* 9 (1979): 442–58. A convenient brief survey that should be supplemented by that of Albert Geritz.

Index

Index

DATE DUE			
FEB 18 1994			

Alist... ...rsity of
Otag... ...erbury,
New ... ...ntario.
He h... ...Souls
Colle... ...sity of
Otago... ...homas
More:... ...n Age:
Humo... ...6), A
Conco... (with
Grego... gns of
Henry... udy of
the Re...